August, 2004

Also by Webster Kitchell:

God's Dog: Conversations With Coyote

Coyote Says… More Conversations With God's Dog

GET A GOD!

More Conversations
With Coyote

GET A GOD!

More Conversations
With Coyote

Webster Kitchell

Skinner House Books
Boston

Printed in Canada

Cover design by Suzanne Morgan
Text design by WordCrafters

ISBN 1-55896-417-7

Library of Congress Cataloging-in-Publications Data

Kitchell, Webster
    Get a God!: more conversations with Coyote/Webster Kitchell.
        p.cm.
    Includes bibliographical references.
    ISBN 1-55896-417-7 (alk. paper)
        1. Coyote (Legendary character)—Fiction. 2. Unitarianism—Fiction.
    3. Imaginary conversations. I. Title.

    PS3561.I843 G4 2000
    813'.54—dc21   00-053815

10 9 8 7 6 5 4 3 2 1
04 03 02 01 00

For Nancy,
our children and grandchildren;
a circle of love
given and received.

CONTENTS

PREFACE

James W. Fowler, in *Stages of Faith,* writes that many of us operate in stage four. Stages one and two are the stages of childhood faith. Stage three is the adolescent experience. Stage four is the midlife faith. In stage four a person has resolved his/her adolescent rebellion and need for authoritative answers. She/he has relaxed into a life. In stage four, we have identities and worldviews that satisfy us. We recognize that our identities and worldviews may be different from those of others, and that's OK with us. We can be critical of our society and our friends and the myths that we were brought up on. It is a time of personal confidence. It is the faith stage that Unitarian Universalists have probably always thought was the goal of life. As a creedless faith that acknowledges wisdom from all the world's religions as one of its vital sources, Unitarian Universalism tends to attract people who want to draw on the rich diversity of religious thought across cultures and history to form a personal spirituality. Unitarian Universalists want the freedom to incorporate contradiction and exploration into their religious lives. They don't want to be told what to believe. As Unitarian Universalists, they are free to be who they want to be.

James Fowler's story of the development of human faith posits two stages after stage four where we linger. Stage five is a place of disillusionment with the rational good life, a time of reflection on all the compromises one has made, on the disappointments and failures of life along with the successes. The person entering stage five realizes the world, the cosmos, and life are overwhelmingly complex and even contradictory. So he or she begins to think of the mythic stories with new appreciation for their nonliteral human spiritual content. The person in stage five has a sweet sense of irony, a sense that with all their contradictions and distortions certain ideas have the ring of truth to them; they are good for all times and conditions. Honesty, for example. Honesty can be painful, so it may have to be tempered with compassion. But still, honesty is a worthy and eternal good. Yet none of us has led an utterly honest life. How do we resolve that? Perhaps through stories of a God who loves and forgives—the Universalist side of the Unitarian Universalist heritage. Maybe it is no wonder that humans created a loving God who knows all and accepts us anyway. Maybe that's a human need.

There is a danger in stage five faith. We see the contradictions of our actions so clearly that we are sometimes paralyzed into inaction and lose hope.

I don't expect stage six of you. It is really for saints, though Dr. Fowler says it comes to more ordinary people than you'd think. Maybe it's a place for retirees! Dr. Fowler writes that stage six people are disciplined and activist incarnations of absolute love and absolute justice. They shake our norms. They threaten what is deemed good and prudent. In situations of oppression, they see clearly what life is meant to be. Martin Luther King, Jr. is the foremost example in our lifetime, but there are uncountable, modest, unsung saints.

Dr. Fowler says, "Religious faith must enable us to face tragedy and finitude without giving in to despair. In our faith we must face ourselves. Our faith must provide liberation and redemption. Truth is a pattern of being; truth is lived."

For Coyote and me, it has meant that we have to live as if the cosmos, the planet, life, our fellow creatures, and ourselves are sacred. That is the myth Coyote and I have returned to.

Webster Kitchell

COYOTE SAYS,
"GET A GOD!"

I was tired. I had spent the day running around doing the errands that seem so important when you're trying to get away from home and can't put them off until tomorrow. My gut was telling me to sit down and relax. So I thought if I put a load of laundry in, *then* I can relax because I'll be doing laundry while I relax. This is known as the compromise between the spiritual imperative to stop and look at the tulips and the moral imperative to improve things until you drop. I put the laundry in and went out on the deck to regard the mountains and a greening-out lilac bush. My emotional needs were in balance then as I meditated, soothed by the sound of the washing machine. I became aware of another presence materializing, and suddenly there was Coyote, with his conspiratorial, comradely smile.

There were no donuts available, ours being a virtuous household, but I was able to rustle up some herbal tea and a package of fat-free vanilla sandwich cookies.

"Is this living?" he asked. "Does it get any better than this?"

"I am depressed and outraged, Coyote," I said. "I have just come from the Taos Film Festival where I saw several good films, but also attended a media symposium. What the television moguls are doing to our culture is scandalous. I think the country is going to hell."

He was not outraged. He calmly said, "Everyone thinks the country is going to hell. Everyone has their own vision of the hell the country is going to. The media are constantly reinforcing the idea that the country is going to hell, and they tell us we should fight back by buying a new pickup truck."

"Exactly my point!" I said. I realized I was not relaxing. I was out of touch with the blooming lilacs in my yard. "George Gerbner,

Dean Emeritus of the Annenberg School for Communications, said humans live by stories. But the stories used to be handcrafted by church and tribe and family and nation. Now the stories of what we should be, how we should live our lives, are being crafted by artists who work for a few media conglomerates that are not interested in our good, but are only interested in selling us what the great corporations want us to consume. Gerbner said, "If I can tell the stories of the culture, I don't care who makes the laws." Humans live by stories.

"I thought that was progress," Coyote said. "Isn't that the story liberals tell? Of how we have made progress over the last few hundred years. Better nutrition, better medicine, better housing, more creative opportunities for fun. Better class of stories."

"That used to be the liberal story," I said. "I think now it's the conservative story. The liberal story now seems to be that we are exceeding the population the planet can sustain with all our progress. Liberals seem to want to curtail progress and conservatives want to see more progress no matter what the cost. It's a reversible world!"

"I thought the electronic media were going to bring in the kingdom of a democratic god," he said. "What happened to all the good debate and free information that was supposed to come with the communication revolution?"

"From what I read in the antiquated print media, it seems to have to do with lobbyists and Congress giving away the farm," I said. "Or rather giving away the power to tell stories that enhance the dignity of being human."

"What stories are those?" he asked.

"They are the stories that your family used to tell about who you could be. They are the stories the church used to tell to show you that your human life was in some way unique and special, even loved by the divine. Now we are told our value is determined by the products we buy and the tourist trips we can afford to take."

"Why did you let that happen?" he asked.

"It happened so fast, we couldn't see it coming," I said. "Democracy is very slow in the way it operates. Maybe democracy only works where people know each other and see each other face to face. Athens or the small New England town meeting or our local church congregations. For Unitarian Universalists, democracy is a sacred way of doing things because we know it enhances the human spirit to be a participant with our fellow humans in deciding our fate."

"As much as you can decide your fate," he said with a wry smile.

"Well, there's another story. Camus's story of Sisyphus. Although Sisyphus was condemned by the gods to meaningless hard labor, Camus said Sisyphus had his dignity because he didn't allow his spirit to be crushed by his fate. Camus imagined Sisyphus happy in his affirmation of his defiant selfhood. That wouldn't be an acceptable story to the mega-moguls of the media. Sisyphus should have capitulated to the gods of commerce by buying a Volvo to boost his self-esteem and show he was a success, by becoming someone whom the media mogul gods had blessed."

"You sure are rabid on the media moguls this afternoon," he said. "Lighten up and enjoy the spring. Let me get you another cup of herbal tea. Have another fat-free cookie! They're good for you."

I relented. After all, why have a minor deity in your life if you can't rely on him to point out your errors and lovingly correct them? We all need that cosmic perspective in our lives. "You're right, Coyote," I said. "I just need to watch a little TV and relax, and I will get over my outrage."

"Sure!" he said, pouring the hot water into my cup and pushing the cookies closer. "Think of all the good TV has done for the cause of social justice. Segregation succumbed to the images on television. The Vietnam War protest happened because of television. Both important political victories for the liberal cause."

"By the Gulf War we had made war a TV entertainment," I said. "I suppose that's progress, too!"

"It's better than being there."

"But it's selective. My son was a Marine Corps grunt doing what Marine Corps grunts always do. He was driving supplies through the desert at night to establish forward bases so the cavalry could make a valiant charge when the time came. The cavalry needs its forward supplies of gasoline, and it's the grunts who get it there. No TV glory for the grunts!"

He gave a cavalier wave of his paw and said, "Never has been glory for grunt work. So what's new about that?"

"I remember a mythic story that used to bring comfort and dignity to the grunts, that the son of God died for grunts, that grunts were loved by God even if they weren't recognized by the human elite who were exploiting them. There was a human story that God cared about us for our sacred selves, no matter whether our hair was clean or our skin was soft."

"Listen," he said, and I knew I was going to hear a true word from my god-friend. "Humans have this dual nature, this inborn spiritual conflict. It is between the spiritual values of resignation, smelling the flowers, and control—what you liberals call "building a better life." Humans experience life as a tension between accepting what they can't change and doing something about what they can make better."

"And wisdom is knowing which is which," I chimed in.

"Let go and let God," he smiled.

"But what about the story of a god who has endowed humans with certain inalienable rights?"

"You can still use the media to tell your story," he went on, like a patient adult explaining to a stubbornly wrong child. "The role of women is changing; not overnight, but really extremely revolutionarily fast given the pace of reform before the electronic media. The acceptance of gays and lesbians has changed radically in your own lifetime. Not into the promised land yet, but we're closer. Life is a dirty mix of needing to make changes, of resistance to changes, of accepting with grace that life is never going to be perfect. So you humans live in the spiritual mix where you tell stories of evil and good, and who wins this round. It depends on your frame of reference."

"How do we get a frame of reference?" I asked softly.

"By getting a god," he said.

"Gods won't fix it," I said. "Gods screwed it up right from the start. You could have made an effortless perfect world." Too late I remembered the story of the Garden of Eden.

Coyote grinned a wide grin with all his sharp teeth and his long, red, saliva-glistening tongue showing. His yellow eyes gleamed.

"You humans made up the story about how you lost Eden. You humans made up the story that perfection is possible. You humans made up the story that Adam and Eve got bored to death with sitting around naked in paradise and decided to eat the apple of knowledge and thus leave the Garden of Eden. A true fable. Be dumb and happy, or get smart and find tragic awareness. Which would you rather?"

"Depends on how my day has been," I said.

"Me, too," he said and drank some tea reflectively.

"You know my favorite story in the Bible?" I asked him.

"What's that?" he asked back.

"David and the prophet Nathan," I said.

"Tell me the story," he said.

"King David was a good king, but he gave in to temptation. He saw Bathsheba up on her roof bathing, and he lusted after her and sent for her. Who was she to say 'No!' to the King? Later Bathsheba sent word to the King that she was pregnant. Now it turned out that Bathsheba's husband, Uriah, was in the army. King David got Uriah a weekend pass, expecting that Uriah would spend it with Bathsheba. But Uriah slept outside the door of his house. When the King asked Uriah why, Uriah said his companions in the army were sleeping on the hard ground, and he couldn't enjoy his wife's bed knowing how his buddies were faring. So the King, good King David, in his absolute power sent Uriah back to the front lines with a secret note to his commander: 'Put Uriah out in front and then pull back and leave him alone.' The commander obeyed, and Uriah was killed. So after a period of mourning, Bathsheba moved her things into the King's palace.

Now in a reasonable, sophisticated society, that would have been the end of the story. But God, Jehovah, was mighty angry. And Jehovah came to his prophet Nathan and said, 'Nathan, go confront the King with the wrong he has done!' It isn't easy being a prophet, a whistle-blower. It's scary to tell the monarch that God is annoyed with him. Nathan approached the King indirectly and said, 'Sire, I have a story to tell you.' King David said, 'Oh, good, Nathan. We love your stories.' Nathan said, 'Well, sire, there was this poor man who had a little lamb, and the lamb was all the poor family had. They kept it in the house and loved it as a pet and it was their sole joy in life. And one day the rich man who lived next door had company to dinner, and instead of killing one of his own two hundred lambs, the rich man took the poor man's lamb and killed it, cooked it, and served it to his guests.' King David was shocked, outraged, angry. 'Who is this man who did such a thing? He must be punished!' And cool Nathan replied, 'Sire, thou art the man!' And David knew that God knew what he had done. David accepted his guilt and did penance, though of course it was too late for Uriah."

Coyote looked thoughtful. Then he said, "I don't suppose you see any resemblance to any contemporary situation, do you?"

"Well, just that some things are always with us."

He pondered. "Why did you tell me that story?" he asked.

"Well, it's one of my favorites from the Bible," I said.

"Why?"

"Because it says there is a transcendent frame of reference that judges the powerful and has compassion for the anonymous humans the people of power—even the good kings—abuse."

"Do you think," he asked, "intelligent people of good will still believe in that transcendent frame of reference?"

"Very few still do," I said. "It's not a story the powerful and intelligent like to hear."

He was silent and thoughtful. I waited. He sighed. Then he said, "Maybe, just maybe, the media are acting as a Nathan come to judgment. Maybe, just maybe, the media that can tell stories of how we are worthless unless we buy the products they advertise could also—at the same time—be the media that bring justice to our society."

I was uncomfortable with this turn of events, but I said, "Well, you could be right. But what would it take to do it?"

"A lot of people who care about their society," he said.

"And how do we find such people?" I asked.

"Well," he said, "first they have to know who their god is."

"And tell the story," I said.

"Do you know any good stories from our time?" he asked.

"Sure," I said. "I know several young women and men who are interns at St. Elizabeth Shelter in Santa Fe. They are learning to work professionally with the homeless. They have a sense of the sacredness of even the most unfortunate. That gives a genuine goodness to their lives. We could do a TV series on idealistic young people!"

"And do they have a god?" he asked.

"I don't know. But they act as though they do. They certainly act as though there is something more important than TV values. They aren't getting rich. They aren't getting powerful. They don't dress and act beautiful. They are good people with an earthy humor and they're pretty happy. They seem to be living what they want to live—a life that transcends their own selves."

He laughed hollowly. "It makes you wonder why they don't get equal time on the news with the murderers and rapists."

"Good stories don't have action, don't frighten people, don't make us so jittery we can't relax."

"What does it take to get that way, to be idealistic?" he asked.

"For some it's an epiphany—a sudden intense insight into the meaning of life. For others it's a long story of the mind reflecting on itself and coming to discover what makes for peace and satisfaction. There's lots of ways people get to it."

"Does it lead to God?" he asked.

"Not always to God, but generally to something transcendent, something that makes one feel intensely that one's life takes place in a larger context than mere entertainment and accumulation. Nice as those things are."

"Are you going to tell your people about this?" he asked.

"I sort of thought I would. Do you object?"

"No, I don't object. But I think telling them about this is sort of like what happened to the Wizard of Oz when Toto pulled the curtain away and revealed it was all a human construct. Wouldn't you do better not to reveal the truth, but to snooker them with smoke and mirrors and pious spin?"

"They're Unitarian Universalists, Coyote," I said. "They know it's all smoke and mirrors. My story for them is that the smoke and mirrors are a necessary part of being human, so they'd better pick humane smoke and mirrors! There are lots of good stories of how to live a life, and they all point to a transcending mystery affirmed."

He looked at me with a simpering look. "And am I really your god?" he asked coyly.

"Some days you are and some days I'm an atheist," I said. "Either way, I'm happy!"

"While you're still in a believing mood," he said, "let's clean up this mess and go for a drive in the desert. It's too nice a day to think such depressing thoughts."

"Thank you, my dear deity friend, for requiring me to perform such a Zen act of devotion," I said. We carried the dirty cups and the empty cookie bag into the house and left them in the sink. Then we roared off to a mountain dirt road, singing gospel hymns loud and off key.

COYOTE SAYS THE GODS
STILL HAVE A FIGHTING CHANCE

t the donut shop I ordered a dozen sugar bombs and two black coffees. Coyote appeared at once and we embraced. I said to him, "It's good to have a god I can count on to show up when I offer sacrifices."

He dipped into the donuts and said, with his mouth full, "It's good to have a faithful follower even if your faith is skeptical. How goes the battle between the self-righteous and the self-doubting?"

I said, "The self-righteous are still self-righteous and the self-doubting are still self-doubting. God's in his heaven; nothing has changed."

"But the Universe still provides us with delicious donuts and strong coffee, so the gods must be good," he said.

I was impatient with being taken for granted. "Don't ever forget, Coyote, I provide the coffee and donuts."

"But we gods have provided a Universe that allows you to exist, for which you owe us a ten-percent kickback, a tithe. Don't you forget that!" His manner was jovial, but I could see the sharp teeth.

"Coyote," I said, and I leaned up against him and laid my head on his furry shoulder. "Coyote," I said again. "Coyote, I would like my struggles with life to *signify*."

He put his paw on my back. "That's why you've got me, baby."

"But how do I know you're not just an aberration of my needful mind?"

"You will never know for sure whether I am or not, but it doesn't make any difference. We'll have another donut and another cup of coffee and enjoy this moment without questioning it."

Oddly enough, I was satisfied and cheered up by his answer. I said, "Paul Tillich used to say something like that. Tillich said humans construct masks of the gods, while the god behind all those masks can never be known. He called it the god behind the masks of God."

Coyote picked up the thought: "We can never be sure there really is a god behind the gods we make."

I took it further: "Our existential plight is that we humans need to live as if there is meaning in our lives."

He didn't miss a beat. He went on: "We create our meaning by living as if our lives have meaning."

I said, a little sadly, "But we never can be sure they do...."

He said, cheerfully, "And we can never be sure that our lives don't have meaning."

I said quietly, "I'd like to be sure."

He said sympathetically, "No, you wouldn't. If you were sure, there wouldn't be any excitement or puzzle or mystery about your life. That's why the Creator of the Universe hides from you."

"So we have to create our own gods?" I asked.

"It's the best way to get a quality god," he said, and he preened a little.

"Coyote," I said, "is it a sign of weakness to ask for a god who wants justice?"

"Not at all," he said, quite seriously.

"Coyote," I asked, "is it a sign of weakness to ask for a god of loving acceptance? Could this god be a Universalist?"

"I think it's a sign of maturity in a god to be a Universalist," he said.

I was feeling bolder. "Coyote, would it be OK to ask for a god with a sense of humor?"

He replied, "There's no one conscious and in touch with the world, including the gods, who doesn't need a sense of humor."

I wanted to be sure. "So," I said, "it's OK for me to have a god that requires justice, accepts humans with love, and has a sense of humor?"

He shook his head with wonder. "Of course it's OK. It's in the Bible, you know."

"It is?" I asked, forgetful. "I thought the Bible was all lawyers and wars."

"Hey," he said. "Remember Micah?"

"Ah, yes," I said. "What doth the Lord require of thee but to do justice, love mercy, and walk humbly with thy god?" I was excited. "So even in the Bible, people made their own gods."

He said, "The gods have evolved along with human awareness. The old tribal gods are uncouth in the modern world. The old gods who saved us by magic are not useful anymore. We need gods who model good behavior for humans. Gods with a sense of irony. Gods with a Universalist acceptance of human inadequacy. We also need gods who get righteously angry, not because they're not worshipped, but at the exploitation of children, at people who get rich exploiting violence and cruelty, at a culture that despises the poor and the weak."

I said, "Making gods is like making music."

He said, "What?"

I said, "Edward O. Wilson, in his book *Consilience,* says that human culture evolves along with genetic evolution. He gives the example of music. He surmises there is probably a gene for music sensibility. Some humans have it strong. They may become composers who can think original music. Then, maybe with a little less strongly developed genetic inclination are the players of musical instruments, whose artistry and hard practice make the thoughts of the composers come alive. Then, somewhat more attenuated, are those who listen to music, the consumers of music. Every individual human has some genetic capacity for music, and the interactions of the composers and the musicians and the people who pay to go to concerts synergistically make the fluid cultural artifact of music. It may be classical symphonic music; it may be adolescent music; it may be music that stirs us to take up arms against another society. The music gene has been rewarded in every human culture."

Coyote signaled the waitress for more donuts and coffee refills. I opened my wallet, but Coyote waved me away, saying, "If you're going where I think you're going with your analogy, I'll buy the coffee and donuts."

I said, "I may be on to a whole new theological approach, where the gods give out rewards for getting it right."

"Try it," he said. "I think we need each other."

So I took an inspirational swallow of fresh coffee and went at it.

"God, if there be a God, is unreachable, at least for Unitarians. The theological endeavor deals with the masks of the gods we humans make. As a culture changes, it creates new gods. The new gods show the people of the culture the changes that are needed. The death of God the Father Almighty, God as Ordainer and Maintainer, the death of that God was the work of atheists and humanists and scientists, people who cared that the image of God the Father didn't work for intelligent people anymore. To use the music analogy, Paul Tillich was a composer of theology. He creatively visualized the existential answer to the modern world's existential dread of its own magnificent meaninglessness. The song Tillich sang was to make the leap of faith as a deliberate self-aware act, knowing it seemed absurd from a strictly intellectual point of view. But it made sense from an emotional point of view. Tillich thought and taught in seminaries. The God retailers, the clergy he influenced, now knew the awful truth: The gods are human creations—with just an off-chance that there might be something behind the creations. The God retailers, the parish clergy, now knew that God seems at best silent and at worst a hoax perpetrated by the elite class and the ruling gender. As a consequence of that new song composed by Tillich and other theologians, and taught by gurus and some progressive clergy, the new young seekers after meaning prefer to look in the silence of meditation, in the still small voice of self-acceptance, in walking archaic mazes. And, of course, another song is also being sung by many humans who find the sacred in caring for other humans, in the struggle for justice and compassion as a way of life, in scientific discovery, in the emotional benefits that come with living democratically, in human intimacy-eliciting groups. In short, in being in human interactions, some of us find the sacred; a mask of God which we think might be synchronous with the god behind the masks of God. But that steps past the bounds of reason into my original emotional wish that my life might somehow signify."

Coyote pushed what was left of the plate of donuts toward me.

"Here," he said, "you earned them."

"No," I said, "not until you answer a question for me."

Coyote looked at the last two donuts as though he were resigned to having to earn one of them.

"What's your question?" he asked, his chin on his paw.

"Are humans hard-wired for meaning? Is meaning something we need to live, or is meaning a meaningless quest?"

"I am not a scientist," he said. "Not because of an inferior mind, but only because of discrimination against admitting non-humans to graduate schools. Think how much more democratic science would be if it included the study by animals of humans."

I felt a touch of guilt, but said nothing.

Coyote continued, "Thus I speak from a lay-deity point of view. Without scientific evidence, it seems logical to me that a need for meaning is hard-wired into humans. Humans who describe them-selves as living meaningful lives seem to be happier and probably enjoy reproducing and raising their children to be good citizens who in turn lead meaningful lives. People who lack meaning in their lives get depressed and miss out on a chance to reproduce that is sitting two rows in front of them right now. So it seems meaning is hard-wired into humans for survival. Besides," he went on, "a sense of meaning can be a great factor in surviving life's very real tragedies and injustices. The god-stories about why there is pain and suffering in life bring solace to the hurting human. They bring your pain into a common bond with everyone who ever lived and hurt. And everyone who lives gets hurt. They answer the question, "Why me, Lord?" with the answer, "So you can learn why love is necessary, buddy."

"Well, so much for the pain," I said. "How about the joy?"

"The joy is in waking up every morning and it's a new day even if it's an ordinary day. The joy is in seeing the sun set and knowing you've met the challenges of the day, even if they were your every-day universal human challenges. The joy is in moments of amaze-ment and wonder when the ordinary flashes with the extraordi-nary, and you feel a rush of irrational gladness. The joy is in having a conversation and suddenly knowing you love the person you're talking to, and why. The joy is in doing life well and being excited about being alive and conscious. Make up your own joys!"

We each reached for one of the last two donuts simultaneously.

"Coyote," I said, "The world of humans needs all the help it can get. Are the gods helping?"

"Dear friend," he said, "we gods are your creations. We will help you if you let us or we will justify violent self-destruction if that is what you choose. But because you created us, we really do exist, we gods. And we are biased by natural selection toward your survival. And what little do we require of you but to do justice, love mercy, and walk humbly together along the path."

I grinned, then whispered, "Would you like to try out my new car on a back road?"

He held out his paw for the key and said, "You trust me!"

"I've never trusted you, old friend," I said. "I'm in this life for the adventure. The car's insured."

"Pay up, and let's go," he said. "And leave a good tip!"

"God told me to leave you a big tip," I said to the waitress as I left $5 by my coffee cup.

"Well, thank God!" she said.

COYOTE WANTS TO KNOW
WHY THE PROBLEM OF GOODNESS

itting on my deck in the cool morning sunshine with a cup of coffee and the newspaper, I was enjoying the goodness of being. I read a story in which a media critic asked some moguls of the entertainment industry if there were some things they wouldn't do. The responses were bluster about artistic freedom and the evils of censorship. Having just sat by mistake through a movie whose whole point seemed to be killing policemen, I thought I had an interest in the entertainment culture.

A spiritual presence began to materialize in the other shady chair. I knew what to do. I went to the kitchen, sliced some fresh bread, got out the marmalade and sage honey, and returned with them and two cups of coffee. Gods and goddesses, even minor ones, must be well fed if one expects spiritual enlightenment. That's something atheists don't understand, which is why they remain atheists.

I said to Coyote, "Let me read you some comments by some big league players in the contemporary culture."

"I'm not interested in your culture," he said and spooned out more honey.

"One said, 'If you don't like my work, you're engaging in censorship, which is a bad thing for you to do.'"

"So why are you doing such a bad thing? Why are you bashing hard-working moguls whose only wish is to appeal to your worst instincts?"

I ignored him. "Another mogul said, 'It's dangerous if anyone feels anything outside the rules is irresponsible and unsafe.'"

"Say what?" asked Coyote.

"If I understand his answer, he means that I'm dangerous if I feel that what's outside the rules is irresponsible."

"So what are the rules for?" he asked.

"My question, exactly."

Coyote mused and sipped his coffee. "I suppose I would have to agree with the mogul. I don't like rules. I prefer chaos. More room for creative encounters."

"Spoken like the Trickster you are."

"Yes," he said, "I suppose there have to be rules for me to do my thing of breaking them."

"Like that story of the stars being set out in a slow, precise fashion by First Man, which you then scattered every which way. So now there is no pattern to the stars as we see them."

He was pleased I remembered. "Looks much better that way." He smiled a smile of creative abstraction.

I said, "I can imagine that there are some humans who would have preferred the stars laid out in rows like the stars on the American flag."

He grimaced. "Sicko people."

"A little order is nice," I observed. "Makes it easier to get through the day."

"You mean everyone out there at rush hour trying to get to work at the same time?" He laughed. "Order leads to chaos!"

I felt I had to say a few ministerial words in favor of order. "These rules were developed over thousands of years of collective human experience and wisdom about what's demonstrably good for people."

He shook his head. "Stupid mistake saying what's good."

"What would you say?"

"Just say what is. Why call things 'good'?"

"Coyote! Bad things do happen. Humans need to know the rules so they can avoid the bad things and work for the good things in life. It's that simple."

"Things are only bad because you say they are bad. A flat tire during rush hour can set you to cursing and damning the gods. But really it's just a thing that happened. Maybe that flat made you miss an accident that might have involved you. Maybe your flat tire saved your life."

"Coyote! Things happen that are *bad,* that people wish wouldn't happen. People live by the rules so there will be less chance of bad things happening."

"No," he said. "Before humans came along with their egocentric idea that the value of things revolves around human wants and needs, there was no good or evil. I am just sitting here in the shade with you, my friend, and we are enjoying a little conversation and some nutrition. That's what's happening. By the way, my coffee cup is empty."

"So it is neither good nor bad that your coffee cup is empty."

He cocked his head. "If you don't fill it, I will dematerialize and you will be left with half a sermon. You being self-centered; I assume you would call that 'bad.'"

I refilled his coffee cup.

I resumed the conversation. "When you are sitting here in the shade eating my bread and drinking my coffee, you agree that is good?"

"Of course it's good. But it's my good. It's not some eternal good that's good for all creatures everywhere in every time."

"What if something were sneaking up on you right now that thought you would be a good breakfast? Doesn't that worry you?"

"Of course it does. Fear is a most useful thing. It keeps us on the alert. Fear is simply an alarm system built into us."

"What if the alarm didn't go off?"

"Well, then I would be breakfast for someone."

"That's good?"

"That's neither good nor bad. That just is! It's just *being* breakfast instead of *having* breakfast."

"I thought you, as a god, would be in favor of some objective divine standards of goodness."

"No! No!" he said, annoyed at my slowness. "The question of good and evil is a question humans have raised. Before humans life simply was. Those who experienced it were glad or sad, occasionally terrified, occasionally deliriously happy. But they didn't make judgments about it. That's the way the gods are. The gods accept that what is is. The gods and the animals alike are puzzled by this human insistence on defining good and evil as though it were something that mattered in the universe."

"Coyote, for people there is the problem of evil. Bad things happen, and people ask, 'Why?' People wonder why the gods made the world this way."

"You're saying that the world would be different if humans had created it? That's blasphemy! That's an insult to the creating deities. Humans have the gall to say the creating deities didn't know what they were doing?"

"Are you saying the creating deities *did* know what they were doing and went ahead and worked evil into their creation?"

"The nature of the universe is change and process. Thus, existence is open to creativity and differentiation and opportunities and possibilities and accidents and excitement. The alternative would be to have a rigidly controlled universe, one with the stars all laid out in a four-square pattern. Some humans are manifestations of a kind of awareness that likes that sort of thing. You and I are manifestations of an awareness that likes the opportunity to change and grow and fashion ideas and things and relationships. The creating deities discussed the possibilities. They also created a four-square rigid little universe in which everything is neat and sweet and nice. It parallels this universe."

I was stunned by this news. "Are you sure of this, Coyote?"

"Of course. All you have to do is believe in it and die. It's called 'heaven.'"

"And you wouldn't want to go to heaven, Coyote?" I was incredulous that I was being told on the highest authority there really is a heaven.

"Of course I wouldn't want to go to heaven. Why do you think I have spent thousands of years on this planet? For the fun of it?"

"You do enjoy it!"

He smiled. "You're right. I do. And so should you humans. If you really lived the way life ought to be lived, you would be full of gratitude for the miraculous surprise of having been invited to the party. You didn't earn this life. You just happened, maybe against your will for all you remember. If it's been pleasurable, well then—wow! If it didn't turn out well, either you were unlucky or you screwed up."

"It still seems evil things happen, Coyote." I was being stubborn, I knew, but I couldn't help myself. It was my outdated cultural programming.

"Evil is not the problem. Goodness is the problem. Goodness makes people stifle their impulses and their joy. Goodness leads to neat arrangements of the stars. Goodness drives people nuts and causes them to sit in darkened rooms with other people and get their excitement vicariously in shoot-em-up movies and erotic fantasies."

"Goodness also causes people to go to church," I said defensively.

"Exactly my point," he said. "They could be out enjoying themselves, but there they are wondering if they're good enough." He was getting excited. "Of course they're good enough!"

"Some people are bad, Coyote."

"That's because they were told as little children that they weren't good enough. You don't see coyotes telling their pups they aren't good enough. You don't hear rabbits telling their bunnies they're evil. Oh, hell, you've left your animal simplicity behind in your quest to be smarter than all other life forms. You are a lost cause!"

We were silent as we pondered that truth. Then he said, "But you make good coffee and good bread. I like your marmalade and honey. If you'd just be satisfied with that sort of blessing, a blessing you have whether you deserve it or not."

"I think I am satisfied, Coyote. When people tell me I 'deserve' something I say, 'I'm not sure I do, but I'll take it.'"

"That's my boy!" he said admiringly. "I think you've got it. Go tell it to the people."

"Some of them are not going to like it, Coyote. They will think it's illiberal, irresponsible, and selfish."

"One animal's meat is another animal's poison."

"So you think it's OK for people to believe in goodness if they need to?"

"Far be it for me to encourage people to change their beliefs. I just think there's more reality involved in understanding the way the world is, not the way it *should be*. I think that's the way to maximize the pleasure of being."

"But, Coyote, good people want to maximize the pleasure for the maximum number of people."

"They want to maximize *other* people's pleasure?" He arched his eyebrow and looked at me with the sort of look I used to get from my parents when I was four.

"It's known as caring, Coyote. It's a human characteristic. Not exclusively, of course. We know other animals care. But we think humans at their best have developed caring to new heights. That is one of the best things about being human—that we care about each other."

"So care about each other. Nothing wrong with that."

"But caring involves some pain, Coyote. Caring people go through bad times with their friends. Caring people worry about the dispossessed and starving. Caring leads to pain."

"Which leads some people not to care because they don't want to feel the pain," he said soothingly.

"Exactly," I said. "Why should caring, which is good, lead to pain, which is bad?"

"Because not caring is worse. You have to discover that for yourself."

I was getting confused about which side he was on. For that matter I wasn't sure which side I was on.

Coyote continued, "The problem of goodness is that goodness leads to pain. We come to understand that pain is a given in this universe of becoming and changing and letting go. The reality of the problem of goodness is resolved by experiencing the transformative power of caring over pain. Thus, caring leads to certain joys that those who defend themselves against caring miss out on. This is what the creating deities learned in making this universe the way it is: open, free, not determined, plastic, and evolving. You and I as living creatures make choices, and these choices create pain and pleasure for us. We can refuse to make the choices, and reality will go on without us. If we refuse to care we may miss the pain of understanding, but we will certainly miss the ecstasy that comes with insight and enlightenment. The lesson life learns—always in an incarnation in a particular life—is to transcend pain and darkness with love and enlightenment. Usually that knowledge comes rather late in life. Your present culture, being youth-worshipping and impatient, expects to know all the answers by age thirteen. Your television takes that as a given. You have no patience with the true meaning of a life—that through long experience and many mistakes, you come to find out what is good about being alive and having the experiences you've had and are still being dealt. If there is any goodness in all that trouble, it is in how you react spiritually in your deepest being to what you are given to overcome, to transcend through understanding and living a life of love."

Then he got stern and seemed self-reflective. We were quiet together for a moment. He continued, "I mean *living a life* of love, not just saying sweet bromides about love. *Living a life* of love is hard and painful at times, but the end result is a transcendence of the selfish and ego-centered idea that the universe was made for you personally. The problem of goodness is that you humans think life should be easy, painless, and shallow. Thus you define a painless, easy, and shallow life as 'good,' and when you don't get it, you get angry and cranky and sulk in front of the TV."

The coffee pot was empty. Our cups were cold. The marmalade jar was on its side and the honey pot was sticky. We had toast crumbs and coffee stains on our fur. We sat there among the ruins of the morning newspaper telling us of rape and larceny and massive indifference to life. The mountains stood as they were. The sun shone down impassively.

Coyote said, "Micah 4:3."

I said, "They shall beat their swords into ploughshares and their spears into pruning hooks; nation shall not lift up sword against nation, neither shall they learn war anymore; but they shall all sit under their own vines and fig trees, and no one shall make them afraid."

We contemplated that for a few moments. Then I said, "I John 4."

Coyote said, "God's nature is active, caring love, and the person who lives in active, caring love is living in God, and God is living in that person."

We beamed at each other, and together went in to the kitchen to see if there was any raspberry jam.

COYOTE WANTS TO KNOW
WHAT A CHRISTIAN EXISTENTIALIST
BUDDHIST HUMANIST PAGAN
UNITARIAN UNIVERSALIST IS

 was at St. Elizabeth Shelter flipping hamburgers at a cookout. There were many coyotes of both genders, including some small coyotes. Mostly they were well behaved and stood in line. Each came to me with a paper plate on which were neatly arranged potato salad and a bun with lettuce and tomato. Just waiting for a nice, hot greaseburger. Then one coyote came up with an empty plate and said, "Give me four!"

"You can't have four, Coyote," I hissed. "Get a bun like everyone else."

"Just what I'd expect from a preacher. Get in line like a lamb. Don't be greedy."

The other coyotes were watching this little power confrontation. I reached over for a bun, put lettuce and tomato on it, and flipped four greaseburgers onto it. There were coyote grins all around at this creative compromise. Coyote moved down the line and grabbed four hot dogs from my unsuspecting co-cook.

"It's OK," I said. "He's with me."

Later we stood wiping the grease from our paws. Coyote said, "You acted like a right-wing Christian minister back there."

"Look, I started out as a liberal Christian: respectable, nothing excessive, straight youthful, innocent idealism. Then I became an existentialist. Then I moved to becoming a humanist, a religious atheist. Then I discovered Buddhism. Now I'm a pagan. I've never been a right-wing Christian."

"Can't you make up your mind?"

"It's not a matter of making up my mind. My mind is only part of it. It's also a matter of imagery, of feelings, of human connectedness. Human connectedness with people alive now, with humans of different cultures, with humans who existed long ago, with humans arriving daily."

"What are you talking about?"

"I went with the cultural program I grew up in until I was in my twenties. Then I had a tragic experience that showed me the good are not rewarded by God. I was shaken to find God silent and indifferent."

"That's when you became an existentialist?"

"Yes. The new insight after the disillusionment came when I read Camus's famous question, 'What keeps you from committing suicide?' If we don't choose to die, it must mean we have something to live for, even if it's only fear of nothingness. So I have been trying to figure out what makes life worthwhile."

"What have you discovered?"

"I'm still working on it."

"You mean for fifty years you've been trying to figure out why life is worth living?" He was incredulous.

I was unembarrassed. "It made life worth living."

"You mean to say all these years you've been posing as a preacher, you haven't known a good reason for living?"

"I've had a lot of short-term good reasons for living. As soon as one would give out, I'd find a new one. For example, one good reason for living was raising children. When that was done, I had a new reason for living. Getting rid of them! When I had accomplished that, I had to make peace with them."

"I know what you mean." We watched several small coyotes picking their hot dogs out of the gravel.

"Did you preach existentialism openly?"

"Oh, yes. It was very popular among certain dissenters who didn't believe in orthodoxy. We were a haven for people who liked church but not what was preached in regular churches."

"So having found the truth, you stuck with it?"

"No. Having found the truth, I questioned it."

"How could you do that?"

"It was easy. I never really threw out my liberal Christianity. So I had three contradictory ideas in my head, and the ideas dialogued in my head as I walked under the shady trees of a midwestern suburb."

"Weren't your parishioners upset?"

"No. They were glad to see the preacher wondered about the same things they wondered about. It made wondering acceptable. Eventually we got relaxed about letting wondering happen openly in church."

"But the truth, man, the truth! What about the truth?"

I quoted Robert Frost: "We dance in a ring and suppose, / While the secret sits in the middle and knows."

He shook his head in disbelief. "So there's no truth?"

"Here's where Buddhism comes in. There is what's true, but it's too magnificent to fit in my skull. We're always wrong, try as we will to know the final answer. There were fourteen things the Buddha refused to discuss because there wasn't any way of knowing them."

"Actually, there are 512 things we can't know!"

"You should know better than me," I said.

"Tell me about the pagan part of your patchwork faith."

"My quilt of many truths," I said reflectively. "I was raised in sensual country with marshes and tides and mosquitoes and severe weather; with barns and woods and long walks down country roads to find my playmates. I left it to live in sophisticated cities, but that rural part of me never left me. Eventually I embraced it and brought it back into my religious hodgepodge. Now when I walk to see the sunset, the sunset is a show of the glory of the natural world. I feel humble and glad to be here."

Coyote put a paw on my shoulder and said, "Cousin!"

I hugged him and thought maybe I'd just stick with paganism and mythic animals.

Coyote said, "But you call yourself a humanist. Aren't you excessively religious for a humanist?"

"There is a barrier around this world of consciousness. Orthodoxy says God can reach through the barrier from the outside and touch our lives. Humanists say the barrier can't be breached. We live within its confines, and within those confines we discover what is good and true for us. I think the humanists are right; there are no revelations from outside, only exploration and discovery."

"So what am I?" he asked defensively.

"You're my exception to the rule. Contradictions are more true than consistency."

"You are more coyote than I am."

"Thank you. I have grown in grace knowing you."

He turned, grinned, and then with a quick motion put a leg behind my knee and pushed me backward. I went crashing down in the gravel. Shocked, I looked up at him.

He grinned.

"Just so you know who's boss," he said and disappeared.

Coyote Says,
"Make Up Your Own Story!"

he morning was gorgeous. I was feeling good. I made some coffee and opened the door to go out for the paper. There stood Coyote.

He said, "You don't want to get the paper; it's full of things that will spoil your day. War and sex—all that stuff that never gets settled, but passes routinely for important in the human mind."

"You used to like sex," I said. "What happened?"

"It's become too common," he said.

"And dangerous to our reputation," I said.

"What's for breakfast?" he asked.

"We could go out for donuts," I said, "or we could slice up some fresh bread I made last night."

"A loaf in hand is worth two dozen donuts in the store," he observed. So we let the headlines languish. We started slicing bread and toasting it and looking for varieties of jam. We made a mess of what had been a neat kitchen. Coyote is an enthusiastic chef, but he is not neat.

Over a thick slice of heavily marmaladed toast and a mouthful of black coffee, I heard him say something that sounded like, "What are you going to do in retirement?"

"I hope to master my computer, for one thing. You know, I just found out, by leafing through the manual, how to generate multiple copies."

"Dear friend," he said, "let me offer you some advice. Don't tell stories unless they reflect well on you. Keep things like that a deep secret."

"I thought we were supposed to be trusting and open," I said.

He reached for another piece of toast and filled his coffee cup. Then he said, in a tone which you get only from a god who is happy with your offering and wants to help, "You *are* supposed to be trusting and open, but not about *everything!* Some things, like not knowing all about your computer, you admit only to your therapist."

"Well," I said, a little abashed, "I trust you. You're my god, and I ought to be able to trust you. I want to be able to trust you." I gave him a big, furry hug.

"Careful," he said, "you'll mess up my tape recorder!"

"You're wired for the FBI?" I asked.

"For the CBI," he said, "the Celestial Bureau of Investigation."

"You mean I'm supposed to believe the gods are recording everything we do? I thought that went out with humanism."

"Only those who are enlightened and know they create their own stories are exempt," he said. "For most humans, we gods record their raw data and assign them a standard story line. But for those who understand that stories give life meaning; well, they craft their own stories and give their own meaning to their lives."

"How does making up a story about your own life give it meaning?" I asked.

"You tell yourself your story. You tell other people your story, filtering what you wish to reveal. You polish your story. You ascribe to yourself good motives and hide your less socially acceptable motivations; you hide your dark and secret shameful wishes. Eventually you will have a story of yourself that will reflect credit on you. You will feel good about yourself."

"What about things that keep coming up that don't make you feel good about yourself?" I asked, a little nervously.

"That's what therapists are for," he said. "They help you put a redeeming spin on the dark side of your story."

"You sure you're not wired and programming me?" I asked.

"My word of honor as a Trickster," he said, "I would never stoop so low!"

"I'll believe you," I said, "because I want to."

"The best sort of reason," he said. "It puts the burden to be honest on others. Even when it doesn't work, it's the best way to deal with trust."

"Or," I said, "you can enjoy being unimportant enough to be inconsequential. Stay beneath the investigators' radar."

"A lot of people lead comfortable, modest lives under that story plan," he said. "It is a recommended procedure for staying out of trouble with the gods. Of course, it doesn't work."

"Nothing does when you're dealing with the gods," I said.

"So skepticism is part of *your* story as a professional representative of the divine," he said. A wicked smile flashed across his face.

I said, "Knowing the story of the divine-human relationship through the ages and across various cultures brought me to a skepticism about faith. But then, eventually, I came to a faith that transcends my own skepticism."

He nodded. "Your own faith wouldn't let you stay in the realm of skepticism."

"Right," I said. "My faith seems more reasonable than my skepticism."

"So," he asked, "how do you resolve this tension between your faith and your reason?"

"By accepting that it is useful to have faith and reason in conflict in my understanding. Faith gives me a perspective in which to do my daily living. Reason uses the facts of my daily living to critique my faith perspective."

"Example?" he asked.

"I was reading an article about the potential flu pandemic that could be a repeat of the 1918 flu pandemic that made the Black Death of the Middle Ages seem minor. Now in the Middle Ages, people assumed this was God punishing a whole population for some biblical sort of sin. From that medieval perspective, solutions involved making scapegoats out of skeptics, witch-hunts. Human reason has progressed enough to say that flu is caused by a virus, and pandemics are caused by modern transportation methods, which allow the deadly flu virus to travel by jet around the globe. The amazing result of human mind power has been to understand the nature of a flu pandemic and try to stop it before it gets started. That's why the chickens of Hong Kong were sacrificed instead of scapegoats. That's a beneficial outcome of generations of human intelligence and scientific cooperation."

"And the faith part of it?" he asked.

"The faith part of it is that certain individual people are willing, for whatever larger reasons, to use their brain power and time and energy to solving this puzzle, either for the pleasure of solving the puzzle or for the humanity of it, or for both."

"Why isn't that reasonable rather than a matter of faith?" he asked, catechetically.

"Because it is equally reasonable to take the position that a flu pandemic is part of a divine plan to solve the problem of human overcrowding and destruction of the planet's ecosystem, and that to interfere with such a planetary cleansing is against the will of God or the self-stabilizing rules of nature. The perspective out of which one reasons is a matter of faith."

"So reason and faith make up a person's story?" he queried.

"There's a third factor," I said. "Life experiences over time."

"Living a life?"

"That's where we test our faith perspective; test its relation to our reason and our experiences, our failures and successes in manipulating life and responding to what happens to us. If we get proficient at living, we probably have good reasoning capacities and a good faith perspective. If we get into new experiences we haven't encountered before, they may lead to a crisis of faith, a crisis that our perspective doesn't work anymore. Hopefully it will lead to a deepening of faith as we struggle through reason with the new life challenge."

He grinned. "Like retirement?" he asked.

"We're working on it," I said, feeling a simultaneous flash of panic and joy.

"Will you work some more on your story?" he asked.

"Of course," I said. "That's what human life is about. Seeing what story we can tell about being alive. Story puts meaning in human life."

"Who listens?" he asked. At first I thought it was a cynical question. Then I realized he was somber and sad.

I started to clean up the mess in the kitchen. Then I stopped and said, "It *would* be nice if you gods would listen and respond with some appreciation of how hard it is to live a life of reason and faith. I guess that's asking too much."

He started filling the sink with hot, soapy water. "You created a deity who works for you."

"So, get to work!" I said.

He dipped a dish towel in the soapy water and snapped it at me. I jumped with surprising speed. "Missed me!" I said triumphantly.

He smiled. There was a cold sureness in his voice as he said, "I'll get you eventually. Never fear."

"Coyote," I said, "Tell me your story."

"You've read my story," he said. "It's in the Native American legends."

"You tell me your story," I said.

He looked reflective, standing there at the sink with suds on his paws. He didn't look like a deity, but he didn't look like he belonged in my kitchen either.

He said, "My story is not your sort of story, because my story doesn't depend on time. My story has no beginning and no end. I come from before space/time beginnings. I will still exist after endings. I am the spirit of becoming. I am the spirit of experimentation. I am the spirit of dark and light mixing to make forms appear. I am the consciousness that loves those forms and wants to understand the passing nature of the forms. I am your judgment that the experience is worth the pain. I am your judgment that the ecstasy is worth the knowing. I am your understanding that understanding is what you do within the mystery that surrounds your understanding. I am the restlessness that you humans call 'creativity,' which existed before the Universe was born, which called the Universe into being with that silent decision to begin. I am your infinite itch that wants to be spiritually scratched. I am the infinite questions that wait ecstatically for the erotic consummation of an answer. I reside in both worlds: the mundane everyday world of consciousness and the craziness of the cosmic spectacle. I am a divine being skeptical of itself. I am the puzzle maker who is ecstatically puzzled."

The kitchen was miraculously clean by this time. We beamed at each other.

"Coyote," I said, "is there any way a mere human being can taste such grace as you have described?"

"There is," he said, "but the cost is pretty high."

"What's it cost?" I asked.

"Giving up the ego," he said.

"But that's what the story's about!" I said. "The story is about the ego."

"Now you know the rest of the story," he said.

"I don't follow your reasoning," I said.

"It's past reasoning," he said. "It is the mystical experience of seeing the stars at night and increasingly understanding what their story is. It is the mystical experience of seeing the human crowds and compassionately understanding that there are all those stories; infinite stories, that if we knew them would make us weep at their pain and *sing* hymns of praise for their bravery and faith and kindness and joy. It is to hear all these stories that the gods were created. We fill a need."

"And how does losing the ego meet these needs?"

"It is a two-step process," he said. "First the ego has to understand that it has no permanence. It is simply a character in a story it tells about itself. It creates itself, yet it didn't create itself out of nothing or in isolation. The ego gains perspective on its own story and acquires a certain realistic humility. This has the effect of either terror at the insubstantiality of our ego or ecstasy at letting go the up-tightness of defending the ego against nothingness. This latter, if it happens, is the mysticism of the no-mind. The union with the infinite. The acceptance of the lightness of being."

I was silent. Then I said, "Yes, I think I understand. But what's the second part?"

"The second part is to return from the mystic experience of the insubstantiality of the ego to rejoicing in being an ego, insubstantial as it is. Because it's ultimately all you've got, and you might as well—literally—make the best of it. You go back to telling your story with the new perspective of your own insubstantiality which is of the same substance as the insubstantiality of the Universe's forms. In our insubstantiality, we are one with each other and one with the Universe."

"Which does what for us?" I asked.

"It opens us up to the magnificent creativity of forms of which our story is a part," he said.

"What if we don't get it right?" I asked.

"That's an ego concern," he said. "There is no right or wrong. There is only the love of being, and being in relationship. The love of being is expressed in very concrete relationships with other forms of being, from animals to stars to mountains to the wind on your face to other human beings."

"And are you a being?" I asked, a little afraid he'd say no.

"We tell stories to each other," he said. "So I guess we leave our tracks in time."

"Coyote," I said, "I think we need to get out in the desert."

"I'll drive," he said.

But that's another story.

COYOTE WANTS TO KNOW
ABOUT THE SEVEN PRINCIPLES

t was a nothing day. Not a bad day; not a good day. Just a day that was insulting my need to feel my sacred specialness. So, I thought, I'll call Coyote and we'll be good for each other. So I got a couple dozen donuts, and when I came in the church, he was waiting for me eagerly. It was going to be a better day, I knew.

He was reading *The Principles and Purposes of the UUA,* which hangs prominently in the foyer. He took a couple of donuts, and with his mouth full asked, "What are these about?"

I said, "Those are the ideals we salute in this congregation. On the sabbath we consider our vision of what human relations should be like on this planet."

"I think we need to talk," he said. "There is no mention of coyotes in there, or of the need to make sacrificial offerings to your deity."

I said, "That will be taken care of in the congregation's mission statement, which we will have ready in a couple of years, God willing."

He said, "God will be willing only if God is included."

I warmed to the task of either converting my deity to Unitarian Universalism or converting Unitarian Universalism to my deity. I said, "The first principle is that we affirm the inherent worth and dignity of every person."

He stuck his long, red tongue out at me and rolled his yellow eyes.

"Come on, Coyote! It's a good ideal!"

"It has to be a realistic ideal," he said. "You can't say there is inherent worth and dignity in *every single human* on the planet."

"Why not?" I asked. "If we all saw the inherent worth and dignity of humans besides ourselves, it would be a better world."

"No, it wouldn't!" he said with exasperation. "Realism says there are valuable souls and there are trash people. There are all sorts of humans, and you have to make judgments and reward the right sort of people and punish the wrong sort of people."

"And who is qualified to make those distinctions?" I asked.

He was incredulous at my stubbornness. "Why," he said, "obviously the good people make those judgments!"

"And who are the good people?" I asked.

"The ones who abide by the rules!" he said.

"And who makes the rules?" I asked.

"The ones who benefit by the rules!" he said. He looked at me as though I was truly out of touch with reality.

"You wouldn't fit in, Coyote!"

"Of course I wouldn't! I'm a deity! The rules don't apply to us."

"Coyote," I said, "this is an *ideal*. This first Principle says how humans ought to be. It's a standard by which we measure ourselves. If we don't honor the dignity and worth of other humans, we are being less than the best we could be. It's a question of being lazy and insensitive to other people, or making the effort to know other people and rejoice in what we find good in them."

"I'll give you that," he said. "But the dignity of *every* person?"

I said, "Sometimes the social machine is designed to take away the worth and dignity of the people in it. Sometimes the social machinery can be designed to *enhance* the worth and dignity of the people in the machine. What I think this 'every person' means is that we can sympathize with the victims of tyrannical regimes and rejoice when people win their freedom."

"How do you create a social machine that enhances people's worth?" he asked.

"That leads to the second Principle: justice, equity, and compassion in human relations."

"How can you include all that in one phrase," he asked. "Justice and compassion are mutually exclusive. Compassion and equity are mutually exclusive. And the way the world is, justice is not always equitable."

"Coyote, don't be such a cynic!"

"Hey, I'm your better half."

I said, "Justice is the way we resolve the conflicts between the inherent worth and dignity of people. We balance the claims rather than suppress the rights of the weaker for the self-interest of the stronger."

He leaned over and said, "Justice is supposed to be blind, right?"

"Yes," I said.

"But *compassion* means *feeling with*. How can you feel with a person and be blind to them at the same time? Similarly, equity implies everyone should get their needs met, but justice suggests that those who work harder should get proportionately more rewards."

I began to wish the subject had never come up.

Coyote went on, "You church people might do well to consult with the gods who made the world and made it unfair. The world was meant to be unfair! That's the way we made it!"

"So," I said, "ideals are a blueprint for improving the world you made! We have had some experience living in your world, and we have some ideas for change. Take justice and equity. That means the quality of the justice you get doesn't depend on who your daddy is. Even tyrants keep up the facade of justice because it deals with the dignity and worth of every person. Justice is an improvement on your 'survival of the strongest' creation."

"How presumptuous of humans to think you can improve on our creation!" he said.

"Unitarian Universalists are always presumptuous in their opinion of the handiwork of the gods," I said.

I went on, "Equity and compassion imply there is a moral wrongness in the present social distribution of the planet's resources. There is also an inequality in rewards for cleverness against those who simply want to live quietly and modestly, just doing their part and enjoying life."

"How does the inherent wrongness get righted?" he asked.

"By non-violent revolution," I said.

"What's a non-violent revolution?"

"Elections," I said. "Democracy."

"Oh," he said.

"Which brings us to the next Principle: acceptance of one another and encouragement to spiritual growth in our congregations."

"Isn't that obvious?" he asked, pouring more coffee. "Isn't that what all congregations do?"

"Some religions don't encourage growth," I said. "They say there is one ancient right way to live and the individual must bow herself to the mores. They say if you're not living right, God won't love you."

Coyote laughed and said, "I love the people in your congregation who aren't living by the code. They're the interesting ones. Tell them Coyote loves the ones who are screwing up their lives for interesting reasons such as exploring things just because their elders said they shouldn't. But why do you encourage them not to live the way their foremothers did?"

"It has to do with their inherent worth and dignity," I said. "There is no final answer to how you should live your life. A healthy radical way of living is to be open to life and learning and deeper understanding."

"But why do they have to accept each other? Why can't they just do it as isolated individuals?"

"Because your experience, if I can get behind your socially acceptable mask, tells me about the variety of ways people experience life, its joys and pains. To know you deeply expands my life."

"I am impressed," said Coyote. "I never knew it was so much work to be a Unitarian Universalist. I thought you were a bunch of people who believed whatever was politically correct ... or nothing!"

"Yes," I said, "compassion and equity are hard work. Democracy and spiritual growth are dangerous freedoms."

He said, "I don't know about this fourth Principle: a free and responsible search for truth and meaning. What would be an irresponsible search for truth?"

"Looking for truth in mind-altering drugs or in revelations from the divine or from dogma that can't be criticized. Maybe the creationists have an irresponsible search for truth in that they start doing their science from a dogmatic conviction."

"Why does it have to be a free search?"

"There are two kinds of truth, Coyote. One is scientific truth, which is based in openness of research, openness to questions, and confirmations by other minds. The second is subjective truth, which resonates with my life experience as a human being trying to live a good life. That needs to be rooted in freedom and responsibility, too."

He asked, "And the search for meaning? Is that different from the search for truth?"

I said, "I find the search for truth gives my life meaning. The search for meaning shows me what's true. In searching for one, we find the other. Because there is always new truth to be discovered as well as new meanings, life is always fun and an adventure."

"What about a good fantasy?" he asked. "Can that be part of a free and responsible search for truth and meaning?"

"I know that's a trick question, old Trickster! Stories, such as this one about a minister who talks with coyotes, can help express truths and meaning. I call them responsible."

He said, "I would have to agree since my existence depends on them."

"Let's move on to the fifth Principle," I said, "which is the right of conscience and the use of the democratic process in society and in our congregations.'"

"Again," he said, "aren't those contradictory? What happens when conscience runs into the democratic process?"

"As we say, Coyote, it leads to another damn growth experience. We have to think it through and feel our way to something good. Hopefully we recognize and honor the dissenter, and the dissenter honors the democratic process and the position of the majority."

"But the dissenter's position doesn't get adopted by the group," he said.

"The difference is that the dissenter gets acknowledged, but does not get to impose his or her will on the group. If he or she wants to remain part of the community, the dissenter cannot claim exemption from the democratic process."

"Does this happen in your congregation?" he asked.

"A healthy UU congregation is one in which people can stand up and dissent and know they will still be held affectionately in the hearts of their community. They may even be honored and appreciated for their dissent. One doesn't have to conform to be valued in this fellowship."

"Try number six," he said.

"The goal of world community with peace, liberty, and justice for all," I said.

"How about a little modesty in your goals," he said. "You want it all!"

"Well, Coyote," I said, "it's one of those things that if you can't imagine it, you can't work toward it. It used to be people thought we had fallen from a perfect human existence. Ours is a forward projection of perfection. It comes out of nineteenth-century optimism, from before science taught us about earth's limits."

"So why don't you give it up?" he asked.

"It gets us idealists through the dark times when we think the greedy and selfish are winning the ideological battles. We think if we can imagine a better way, we can find the strength and courage to work for a better way. Arguing about ends gets us nowhere. Agreeing on the ends and arguing how to get there leads to creative breakthroughs."

Coyote smiled and said, "Isn't life a wondrous blend of fact and fantasy, of goals and tools, of building blocks and dreams?"

I said, "You gods gave us imagination and real hard limits. That forced us to develop creative minds and creative relationships and human culture. Good thinking on your part!"

"It has been entertaining for us gods to watch."

I said, "But it ends up with people not believing in you anymore. No more sweet-smelling offering of ox steaks."

"The priests made up all that about blood sacrifice," he said. "The gods are vegetarians."

"That should be news to the Christians," I said.

He said, "What the gods want and what humans imagine the gods want are very different. But as you say in your Principles, we mustn't interfere with the free and responsible search for truth and meaning by giving out the answers in advance. You have to discover them for yourselves."

"Which leads," I said, "to the seventh and favorite Principle of the Unitarian Universalists."

Of course he knew it. " 'Respect for the interdependent web of all existence of which we are a part.' My favorite, too," he said.

"This is the one we howl in unison for, Coyote. This one sums up all the others. This is the mystical basis for the other six Principles: respect for the interdependent web of all existence of which we are a part. That's the basis for the inherent worth and dignity of every person. That's the rationale for justice, equity, and compassion. That's the meaning in accepting one another and the why of spiritual growth. The seventh Principle came to us through a free and responsible search, and thereby we have found spiritual meaning for our lives. That's why conscience and democratic process are so important! That's the human vision of a society that includes peace, liberty, and justice. I say we are beholden to everything that is; that there is no certain distinction between life and non-life, no distinction between fire and ice as the end of life and the re-creation of new forms. The seventh Principle is a new paradigm, even for liberals, to understand there are real limits and there are creative possibilities."

He asked plaintively, "And is there room in all that for an old coyote?"

I replied, "For us this is the mystical vision: a universe in which everything is interdependent. So there's room in it for an old coyote and an old minister and endless conversations."

"You are getting embarrassingly close to the truth," he said.

"You can have the truth," I said. "I'll settle for some meaning in a universe some think is meaningless."

He stood and gathered the donut sack and coffee cups. Then a quizzical expression came on his face. "How did you Unitarian Universalists come to these seven Principles? Did they come as a revelation or on plates of gold?"

"Believe it or not," I said, "they are the work of a committee. A committee that sent out surveys. A committee report that was voted on at two General Assemblies. Democratic process all the way!"

"You can't fool me," he said. "Theology isn't done that way!"

"It is here!" I said.

"It's a miracle," he said. "I believe you!"

"You better believe me or no more donuts," I said.

"I am your faithful servant," he said, and we both laughed at that idea.

COYOTE CONSIDERS BECOMING
A UNITARIAN UNIVERSALIST

oyote appeared while I was in the kitchen cleaning up some dirty dishes someone had left as a gift to the staff. He said, "Here, let me help you with that."

"Is this some of your work, Coyote?"

He was shocked. "I always clean up my messes!"

"And make a bigger mess."

"Oh my, aren't we in a bitter mood this morning?"

"Right! Cheer me up!"

"I'm thinking of joining your church!"

Without thinking I said, "You can't, Coyote. It's for people."

I could see I had hurt him. I felt a rush of remorse. Gently I said, "You're a god, Coyote. Gods can't join churches."

"Why not?"

Faced with the question, I didn't have an answer.

He said, "I've been looking into it. The Jews let their God join the temple."

"That's different. They have a covenant. They are supposed to be grateful to Him, and He's supposed to look out for them. Then they argue about who has let the other down."

"You mean the Jews argue with their God?"

"Just the way you and I argue. That's the way it is supposed to be between a god and humans. Creative arguments. 'You promised!' 'But I'm God!' 'You promised!' 'Well, you sinned!' 'We're only human. Forgive us.' That sort of thing."

"That's the reason I want to become a Unitarian Universalist. I get to argue with you all the time. I sort of know where you are. I want the opportunity to argue with all those nice, intelligent people in the Santa Fe UU congregation. I don't want to have to go through you all the time."

"Coyote!" I said, "That's why I am ordained! So I can talk to you on their behalf. If they believed they could talk to you directly, where would I be?"

He saw my point. "Maybe you could be moderator."

"No, Coyote, I don't think that would work."

He looked at me with suspicion. "You're not being straight with me. There's another reason, isn't there?"

There's no sense trying to hide things from your god. That's the point of having a god; you can let it all hang out to dry and be forgiven. I was caught in the vise of honesty and was being squeezed.

"Yes, Coyote, there's another reason." I implored him with my eyes not to ask.

He turned the handle of the vise. "What is it?"

I threw myself on his mercy. "Some of our members are prejudiced against gods." The truth was out.

"But there's a plaque in the foyer saying you're a Welcoming Congregation!"

"That just means we welcome all sorts of *humans,* Coyote. Some of our members have had bad experiences with other gods and are prejudiced against all gods as a result."

"Why have a church if you don't have a god?"

"They want the good things you get with a church without the demeaning relationship that's implied in having a god."

"*Demeaning relationship?* What are you talking about? Don't we have a nice, furry relationship? Don't you feel warm and safe in my company?"

"I'm not talking about us, Coyote. It's just that some people have a problem with a god in their life."

"How do they get mystery and holiness in their lives?"

"They think holiness and mystery are really mystification. They think mystification is a sin. They want to bring mystification into the piercing spotlight of rational science."

"Did you say sin?"

"Yes, they think it's a sin to imagine spiritual powers."

He said softly, "This congregation needs me. Can't you see me at a potluck knocking people's plates to the floor and saying, 'Now do you believe in God?' Can't you see me coming to the Theology

Group or the Philosophy Group? They'd sit up and take notice if a real furry god with yellow eyes and big sharp teeth walked in to lead the discussion. See, the trouble is the gods have let this disbelief get out of hand. All they had to do was show up occasionally and go 'Rowf! I am your god.' I'm going to start a campaign among the lesser gods to put a little fear into humans. People need to know all this creation and life didn't just happen by itself."

I was getting nervous that some church members might show up and try to join the conversation.

"I hate to tell you this, Coyote, but a lot of humans here think creation really did happen all by itself." I turned on the dishwasher while I tried to break the news. "We are tolerant, Coyote, but we have our standards."

"Show me a copy of your standards."

"They are invisible boundaries, Coyote. You can't see them, but you can feel them when you run into them."

"Other congregations write them down. Commandments! They let you know what you're signing on for when you join them. You're saying you've got rules, but they're secret. That's not fair! I'm not sure I want to be a member of this congregation!"

I sighed a silent sigh of relief. I could see him running for president of the Board.

"Coyote, here's how it is. We don't write down our rules because rules that are written down are hard to change. We want to be able to change for changing conditions. A congregation that wants to keep the eternal verities has to be flexible and open to emerging new truths."

He started to spin and was disappearing.

"Wait, Coyote, don't go! We need you! Come back!"

He stopped spinning and looked expectant.

"We need you to be our god, Coyote. Not a member. Your duty as our god is to play tricks on us that keep us thinking, unsettled. Like all humans, we tend to think we have all the answers and that makes us intolerant and arrogant. Your job is to sneak up behind us and set off a firecracker. Just keep on being Coyote and we'll keep supplying the donuts."

"Let's get out of this kitchen and get to the donut shop!"

"My treat," I said.

"At the church's expense," he said.

"They think you're worth it!" I said and hugged him.

He whispered in my ear, "I am!"

COYOTE IS NO PACIFIST,
BUT HE IS WILY

I hadn't seen Coyote for a while, and I felt the need to be with him. I went to the sacred place, said the sacred words, and the magic happened once again. He had a new haircut. The top was long, but the sides were shaved.

"What have you done?" I demanded.

"I have become radically apolitical." He squinted at me as he finished the first three donuts. "You need a more contemporary haircut," he said. "You look like a liberal. Shave your head."

"I am a liberal! Raised as one, been one all my life, always will be! Besides, I need every hair I have."

"That's a pretty conservative attitude," he said in a judgmental tone. "We apolitical types are able to blow with the wind, whatever is current."

I looked him over for body-piercing adornments. He read my thought and said, "Doña Coyote wouldn't let me."

"I'll bet you're grateful."

He laughed and held his coffee cup out to the waitress to be refilled.

"You are so right!" he said. "You read me as though we were twins."

"Which of us is the evil twin?"

"You are, because you are a clergyperson and think yourself liberal and therefore morally superior."

"That makes me evil?"

"Of course. We apolitical neo-hedonists are the only truly sincere and morally consistent beings."

"You better be careful, Coyote. Religion and morality are coming back into style. You may find the fashion winds blowing in your eyes."

"Religion is irrelevant. Science has conquered all that. Idealism is situation ethics pretending to be truth established on a rock."

"The pendulum is swinging, Coyote. It will bash your unprotected flank."

"Ah, life is an endless succession of sugared donuts. Eat them before they get stale! There will be fresh ones baked overnight. Science has determined there is continuous re-creation of pleasure."

"Interesting," I said. "A recent survey showed that many scientists still believe in God. A survey was done in 1916 which found that forty percent of biologists, physicists, and mathematicians said they believed in a god who, in the survey's words, 'actively communicates with humankind and to whom one may pray in expectation of an answer.'"

He was amazed. He thought, and then his eyes lit with a holy light. "You mean they believe in me?"

"Well, they believe in someone."

"What about the other sixty percent?"

"Fifteen percent claimed to be agnostic or have no belief. Forty percent said they didn't believe in the god specified in the survey. So we don't know if they believe in some other god image. The assumption of the psychologist who did the original survey in 1916 was that as scientific knowledge increased, there would be a reduction in belief in God. The original psychologist was a devout atheist and predicted that as education spread, disbelief in God would grow. Eighty years later, using the same instrument and a similar random sample, the belief in God among scientists has remained essentially the same."

He licked some sugar from his plate. "So what does that prove?"

"Simply that atheists can be as wrong as Billy Graham in their predictions of converts to their faith."

"What else?"

"Only that so-called hard scientists like mathematicians and chemists tend to be more devout. Soft scientists, such as anthropologists and psychologists, tend to be less devout. The speculation is that hard scientists like definite answers."

"Even if wrong?"

"Who's to say they're wrong?"

"The psychologists and anthropologists?"

"They're guessing, too."

He looked winsome. "But you still believe in me, don't you?"

"Of course," I said, as reassuringly as my doubt would let me.

"I wonder why humans are becoming more conservative instead of more intelligently liberal," he mused.

"People are getting fed up with permissiveness and tolerance. They think it's time for transcendent standards for human conduct, along with a little divine repression of sin. At least for other people."

"Who's doing the defining?"

"Until recently it was the conservative Christians on one side and the Green Party on the other, with the liberals in the middle seeing the appeal of both."

"I thought you liberals were going to sweep the world with your sweet reasonableness."

"There was a time when we hoped we would. We felt we were so right we couldn't help but win the world."

He meditated, and then he smiled. "Maybe, just maybe, the reaction to liberalism on the Right and the Left proves that you really are a threat. Maybe it proves you're succeeding!"

"Ah, you know how to cheer up your client!"

Graciously he said, "What's a god for if not to agree with you when doubt assails your spirit?"

"You lead me beside still waters and prepare a table before me in the midst of my enemies. You restore my soul!"

"Just look at all you liberals have accomplished. You have contaminated the youth, so they are cynical about patriotism. You have brought women into the clergy, destroying the sanctity of maleness. You have television sitcom heroines coming out. You have made divorce and abortion respectable. You have made sex a recreational activity even for adolescents. You have made it OK not to attend church. You urge the underclasses to protest their plight. You have been ingenious in redistributing the wealth, thereby creating a huge middle class that rejects your liberalism. You have made it acceptable for men to have midlife crises in which they question keeping their noses to the grindstone until the day of their death. You have made war impossible through domestic reaction to real blood on TV. Congratulations on your liberal achievements!"

I sat stunned. I had never heard our accomplishments put quite that way.

Coyote continued, "So, such success has to expect a little reaction, a little repression."

"You are something of a cynic, Coyote."

"I've been around a long time, and I've seen a lot. Idealists tend to fool themselves into thinking things have to be perfect before they're OK. Anything less than perfection leaves them unsatisfied."

"You have my interest," I said. "Give me an example."

"Justice Felix Frankfurter once remarked, 'It is a fair summary of history to say that the safeguards of liberty have frequently been forged in controversies involving not very nice people.'"

"But it was good people who forged liberty!"

"It was a mixed bag like everything else in the universe."

"But, Coyote, it's the good people, the moral people, the idealistic people who have brought progress like individual liberty."

"Yes, and they have wreaked havoc!"

I whispered, "Coyote, don't let this get out, or I will be out of a job, and you will be out of donuts!"

"Never fear. Even if you told them from the pulpit, they wouldn't believe you."

"So, freedom has its limits?"

"Even for the gods," he said.

I said, "Try war and see what you come up with."

"I see idealists justifying war, so people will lose their common sense and basic animal humanity. Give people a modestly comfortable life and a little freedom so they're not bored by the tedium of life. They will marry their neighbors, or at worst ignore them. Bore them or impoverish them or deny them basic justice, and they will be easy prey for propagandists for an idealistic war."

"But everyone says being warlike is human nature. You're saying it's not human nature?"

"You're animals, right? Do you see animals going to war?"

"No, but they prey on the weak in the food chain."

"But that's not organized warfare. That's just staying alive. It's highly personal. Part of being alive. Nothing to take seriously."

"Lots of people take it seriously! They think it's wrong."

"My dear reverend friend, they are idealists in a real universe. The food chain is lunch. War is a deviation from the human animal nature masquerading as idealism."

"Sometimes it's self-defense, Coyote."

"Ah, self-defense is fine. A lunch has the right to a defense. A people threatened by warlike idealists has the right of self-defense."

"You may be convincing me, Coyote, but I doubt I can convince the congregation."

"The aggressor always has to cover his aggression with honeyed phrases. Hitler didn't say, 'Let's turn Europe into a fiery hell for the fun of it.' No one would have come to his war. America didn't say to its children, 'Let's go kill the Vietnamese for the fun of it.' Humans are too decent and modest in their animal nature to do that. It's only when they are stirred up by an idealist that they go bad."

"Maybe this has something to do with what we were discussing about atheists a while back."

He was alert. "You're not going to pin a bad rap on me!"

"Not at all. I value you because you are a wise and cynical and skeptical spirit guide whom I trust almost as a part of myself. I tend to believe you. I just wonder if maybe most of the gods of humans have been used by their worshippers to justify self-righteous sins."

"Such as your captains of industry piously telling you they know God knows they must be better than you because they have been so richly rewarded by God?"

"I hadn't thought of that, but now that you bring it up, why yes."

"Again," he said, "humans' ego needs are more than their modest animal needs. The other animals know how to coexist within the reality of the food chain."

"Are the animals atheists?" I asked.

"Of course!" he said. "Only humans believe in God—an extension of the colossal human ego. Having to be one with the purpose of the universe."

"Are you a creation of excessive ego?" I asked with a pretended innocence.

He was indignant. "No, no, of course not!"

"Then what are you?"

"I am your better natural nature, your animal nature, your inner better nature with whom you dialogue, even as we animals dialogue with our inner spirit when the sun is warm, and we have had a good lunch, and there's nothing stalking us. Then for a brief moment we are glad to be alive and give thanks to our creator."

"You're quite sure there is a creator?"

He looked offended. "Of course there's a creator. We wouldn't be having this conversation if there weren't a creator. And a wonderful creation it is, too!"

"But you said the animals are atheists."

"The animals do not believe in the god of the human ego. The animals thank the creator of their animal nature."

"Coyote, where would I be without you?"

"Chairman of the Joint Chiefs of Staff? Speaker of the House? With your ego needs, you could have been president."

"Thanks a lot, Coyote!"

"You owe me big!" he said.

COYOTE WANTS TO KNOW
WHERE HUMANITY IS GOING

ome stuff for the rummage sale was piled up in the church storage shed. I dragged a black sack of it up the steps, only to be greeted by Coyote.

He was excited. "Look what I found!" he said. And sure enough, it was exciting. He had found a Ouija board and a murky crystal ball. We took them back to the church kitchen and cleaned them up.

Coyote said, "Let's give 'em a try!"

I said, "We'd better go in my office and lock the door. I think the congregation would be shocked to see the minister with a Ouija board. It's all I can do to get them to accept you, old friend."

So we made some coffee and concocted some nachos from the darkest recesses of the refrigerator and went into seclusion to bring you this report on the future of humanity. You have to understand that past performance does not guarantee the same rate of return in the future, and there is an inherent risk in fantasizing the future of humanity.

We started with the Ouija board.

"How does it work?" asked Coyote. "I don't see any place for batteries."

"It works on spiritual energy," I said. "We ask it a question with our paws on this little sliding piece, and the spiritual energy spells out an answer."

So we each put both front paws on the Ouija board, and I asked, "Where is humanity going?"

The sliding piece slowly moved our paws to these successive letters: w-h-e-r-e-d-o-y-o-u-w-a-n-t-t-o-g-o.

"What kind of an answer is that?" I said.

"Simple," said Coyote. "It says, 'Where do you want to go?'"

"That's no answer," I said. "That's just answering a question with a question."

"Predicting the future's like that," he said.

"You mean it's up to us humans as to what humans will evolve into?"

"I think that's the terrible truth," he said, with a sadistic grin lighting up his shaggy face.

"I was hoping for a magic solution," I said. "Magic solutions are so much more pleasant and involve a lot less work. Couldn't we just pray for a miracle?"

"You wouldn't like it if you got one," he said. "Most miracles have unintended side effects."

"So," I said, "the humanist rationalists are right. We are gaining control of our own destiny and cannot blame the gods anymore for what happens to us, nor expect them to intervene and save us."

"The old Ouija board never lies," he said, with that complacent, knowing, maddening grin on his ugly realist face.

"Take me back to the Middle Ages," I said, "when prayer was believed to be effective in such hard times."

"It's a mix," Coyote said. "Take El Niño, which is being blamed for everything wrong in the world. Is it partly an effect of there being too many humans on the planet? Or is it a completely natural phenomenon unrelated to human presence? Can we develop technology to lessen its impact on our lives? Can we predict when it will happen and allow for it, prepare for it? Can we use our collective intelligence to help us survive natural changes in the environment?"

He went on, "I think you humans prefer to blame El Niño for disasters the same way people blame their family of origin or their spouse for their unhappiness. The advantage of such irrationality is that people don't have to face up to their responsibility for their lives despite life's perilous setting. People want life to be fun and effortless."

I said, "But we can't be responsible for everything! We may be responsible for our own well-being and happiness quotient, but we can't take on everything. Some natural conditions are out of our control. Some human factors, such as nuclear pride and corporate maximization of profits, aren't under our control either. It's not fair to put the whole burden on one informed, well-intentioned individual."

"We asked the Ouija board what is in the future for humanity, not for you, personally," he said. "Humanity, if collective humanity wants to survive, needs to start taking responsibility for itself."

"But individuals aren't humanity," I said, puzzled at what he was getting at.

"You humans are too much concerned with your individual lives. You are going to have to give up a little of your individuality if your species is going to survive. We coyotes are adaptable as a species as well as individuals. At a level you don't understand, we are able to adapt and survive. If we're threatened with extinction, we have more pups. If there are too many of us, we have smaller litters. You humans adapt and use your clever new ideas to get more personal control and satisfy your greed or your personal security needs."

"So we have to give up being individually fulfilled and become planetary tribalists?" I asked.

"That's not the only answer to the harsh reality that humans have only humans to rely on for survival," he said.

"Name me one other," I said, getting quite depressed at the idea of submerging my beautiful individuality I had worked so hard to create, submerging it into the common good of the mass.

"A certain amount of individuation is necessary for life to have meaning," he said. "But there is a tendency to carry it too far into isolation and greed. Some individualism is important because holiness (and that's the purpose of humanity—to discover what holiness is) is felt in its highest form as the individual feeling herself or himself ecstatically alive and one with the universe. But that sort of mystical excitement about being alive is a jewel in the setting of human culture. It is most especially true in this time of the rational scientific humanist culture, which is typified by intelligent, open, intellectual sharing and interchange of ideas and a certain common commitment to a better life of the human mind. That involves freedom for the mind and education and a fairly benign society where human intelligence doesn't have to be consumed with protecting itself against other human intelligence."

"Such as preparation for war," I said.

"Preparation for war is the most obvious," he said. "There is also ideological aggression and economic imperialism and armed ignorance in the streets. Those, too, are cultural creations of human intelligence."

"So if I understand you, if humanity is to survive, let alone have a chance to evolve, we need to unite our extravagant intelligence in an awareness that goodwill between people is not a luxury nor a sentimental sweetness, but is hard-as-nails necessary for our survival in a harsh world."

"Yes," he said, "I think that's what the Ouija board had in mind."

"Blaming the gods won't help," I said.

"Not a bit," he said.

"Prayer won't do it," I said.

"Sorry," he said.

"Blaming selfish humans won't do any good," I said.

"It may relieve your own guilt, but it won't add a whit to the survival of the species," he said.

"Being intelligent and good is the only way," I said.

"It guarantees nothing, but at least it offers a chance," he said.

"Let's try that crystal ball," I said.

So Coyote burnished the cloudy old crystal ball on his furry chest, and we looked in it. Of course we could see our reflection. Coyote explained that all crystal balls show on their surfaces reflections of the creatures using them, and we had to try to see further down into the cloudy crystal ball.

An image began to appear. It was murky and out of focus. It seemed to be a meeting of some humans. Suddenly Coyote, with his superior insight and sensitiveness to co-tricksters, understood what we were seeing.

"It's the State Board of Education," he said. "They're discussing whether creationism as a theory is on a par with evolution as a theory, and that therefore in fairness to religion the two theories should be taught, because the important thing in education is not the truth but the rights of organized constituencies."

"How's the argument going?" I asked.

"I think evolution is winning since the recent election," he said, squinting.

"Why is that important to humanity's survival?" I asked.

"Because you can't expect to survive if you don't first have a firm grasp of reality," he said as though he expected me to know something that basic.

"I take it you're in favor of excellent universal education," I said.

"What else could I be for?" he asked, indignant.

"Some tricksters are for undermining education and censoring education and denying education because it's too expensive for large taxpayers who are having to make do with three cars. I think they're just afraid of an intelligent electorate."

"If you listen to those tricksters they will successfully eradicate your kind. Which might be called justifiable self-extinction."

"Hit the remote control on that crystal ball," I said.

Another fuzzy picture appeared deeper in the ball than our anxious reflections. It seemed to be a ship releasing a balloon. I said, "I know what that is! It's scientists investigating the loss of the ozone layer."

"Right!" he said. "After education, there's the scientific community of humans networking to examine the planet and trying to understand how it keeps itself naturally renewed and what you humans are doing to that natural balance."

The crystal ball had cleared slightly, and the picture changed again. This time the scene was a group of humans sitting around on chairs in a circle. They seemed very intent on each other. "What are they doing?" I asked Coyote.

Coyote closed his eyes and seemed to tune in on the discussion in the crystal ball. He began to smile and nod his head. He opened his eyes, and whispered, "They're a support group. They are helping each other with their emotional problems. They are dealing with unhappy feelings and their anger responses to not feeling loved. Because they listen to each other and care, they are feeling good about themselves and loving toward other people. Some of them can even begin to believe that they personally are lovable and good and worthwhile."

"This is getting radical, Coyote," I said.

"If this is radical," he asked, "what are conservatives trying to conserve?"

"Let's see if we can see what needs to be preserved."

Once again we looked into the crystal ball, and this time we got a rather clear picture of the signing of the Declaration of Independence. "Why is that in there?" asked Coyote.

"Because it shows people taking responsibility for the kind of government they have. If we are going to survive, citizens have to take part in the political process: vote and lobby and support candidates. To be conservative should be to conserve our freedom, to insist that our elected leaders do what needs to be done for humanity to survive. To be conservative is to take a long view of the consequences of political acts. To be conservative is to conserve what has been good in human culture (learned the hard way over time) and improve on it."

He said, "I thought conservatives were against anything new."

"Sometimes they seem that way," I said, "but I consider myself a conservative in that I want to conserve the planet for future life, conserve the possibilities for a good human life by the intelligent and enlightened use of new information."

"But how do you know what information is going to be good information, and who's intelligent enough and enlightened enough to say how we'll use it?" he asked.

"That's why the crystal ball is clouded," I said. "That's the excitement of the future."

He said, "I notice a lot of pessimistic faces on intelligent and enlightened and kind people. If it's exciting, why aren't they excited?"

"Many of them have grown bitter, Coyote, from fighting for their ideals and thinking they would see their ideals realized in their lifetimes."

He was quiet; then he said, "So this is a long-term project."

"Survival is a continual project," I said. "It is never completed. There are environmental limits that we maybe can't control. We need to discover them and accept them. And there are the threats the human presence presents to humans. Every species has a predator that keeps it in check. Humanity is its own predator. We will limit ourselves either through human madness such as genocide and mass starvation and disease or perhaps we will learn to limit ourselves through intelligent self-control."

"Has any species ever been able to do that?"

"Not that we know of. But that doesn't mean it's inevitable that we will self-destruct. The future looks ominous and harsh, and that's reality. Humans are getting in touch with that reality. It depresses some and energizes others. But human intelligence and interconnectedness are growing realities, too. That's a reality as well."

He smiled and asked, "Would you care to make a prediction about how it will turn out?"

"I would not," I said. "For two reasons. One, the interplay of the destructiveness of the human presence and the inventiveness of human intelligence is too complex to predict. Second, it's a rolling frontier, a continuing crisis that will never end. We will never be able to relax and say we're safe as a species for the rest of time."

We were silent, each with our own thoughts. Then he said, "As a god, I don't know how I'd like to see it turn out."

"That's why we can't count on you," I said. "We have to grow up and take responsibility for it ourselves. You gods are uninvolved observers."

He said, quietly, "Not so. Let's look in that crystal ball again."

So we looked into the crystal ball again. Of course, on the surface we saw our own reflections. But in the murky depths of the clouded crystal ball was a bright spot. And do you know what we saw there?

We saw caring individuals joined together in congregations like ours.

COYOTE ASKS,
"IS THERE ANY HOPE?"

fter closing the ministerial sanctuary, I went to the donut shop. I ordered two coffees and a dozen jelly-filled donuts. As I knew it would, this offering to the gods paid off. Coyote materialized, scarfed down several sugar bombs, slurped the coffee, leaned back on his elbows, and eyed me.

Genially he asked, "What do you need your favorite deity for today?"

"Ah," I said, "I have to go to Houston."

He looked concerned. "What have you done that you have to go to Houston?"

"I haven't *done* anything," I said defensively. "Going to Houston isn't punishment."

"Then why go there?"

"Some important people asked us to come. They want you to come, too."

"Me? Go to Texas? You are supposed to attract Texans here. Texans are New Mexico's cash crop!"

"We have missionary work to do, Coyote. We have to demonstrate to the people in Houston that there is still hope."

"There is?" he said, surprised. "Where is it?"

Now this is not the response one wants from one's god. Pension and Social Security suddenly appealed to me. I had a coffee refill and one of the sugar bombs. I didn't have enough long-term optimism to order a low-fat muffin. Discouraged, I said, "I find myself more and more sympathetic with the churchmen who threatened Galileo when he challenged the three-story universe."

He nodded. "You've got to stop reading Stephen Jay Gould. Gould will take away your belief that you humans are the delight of the gods. The gods are supposed to see that you humans come to no harm despite your selfish and arrogant human behavior."

"I don't harbor the illusion that humans are the delight of the gods, especially after hanging out with you, my semi-divine friend. I know you are only in it for the sacrificial donuts. I respect you for that. You are an honest-to-God honest god."

I am flattered," he said. "But I am in it for more than the donuts. I love you, you know."

I blushed, but I was not to be seduced. "That doesn't mean you'd save me," I said.

"Save yourself!" he said, though not in an unkindly way. He took the last donut.

I went on. "What Stephen Jay Gould says in *Full House* is that we can't even take comfort in the old belief that we are the cream of the evolutionary process. While Unitarian Universalists haven't believed for a long time that we were created by God especially to have dominion over the earth, still we believed in what we thought was the natural evolutionary progress onward and upward forever. We were able to get around not being the darlings of the gods from day one of Creation by saying we must have been meant to evolve into becoming the darlings of the gods. Tielhard de Chardin was probably the best theological theoretician of this idea, but Unitarian Universalists are the prime, actual, practical believers of the idea that humans are evolving into the most intelligent life in the universe."

I heard Coyote mutter to himself, "These humans are too intelligent to believe in God even when One pulls the chairs out from under them just as they were going to relax and sink into contemplation of their own glory."

I said, "Gould managed to do just that on your behalf. He pulled the chair out from under us and laughed when his fellow humans fell on the floor. Gould says we probably saw the progressive drawings in our high school biology text that showed life getting more complicated in the sea, and then crawling on the ground, then learning to stand on two legs, and then (drum roll) *homo sapiens* appeared wearing Birkenstocks!"

"Who do you think drew those pictures?" he smirked.

"I'm quite sure it must have been a human being."

"The probability is high." Then he said, "If you want to keep this relationship going, you need to sacrifice some more jelly-filled donuts."

"I am your attentive minister," I said, and signaled the waitress.

Coyote went on with the thought. "Yes, a human being drew those pictures. Totally objective, right? Obviously to a human the human is higher, higher is up, and that puts humans on top. All sensible animals would agree, once it had been pointed out to them, right?"

"Even a coyote."

"Coyotes know that people find what they are looking for. If you're looking for a spurious claim that you are special, you'll find one even if you have to make up the evidence."

I said, "Gould wonders why our textbooks never consider that intelligent life might not have wanted to come onto land. Maybe there was an evolution of intelligent beings who preferred to stay in the sea."

"Don't tell people that. They won't be able to handle it. They have to believe that working in tall buildings and driving freeways in air-conditioned private pods is one of the greatest things that's happened to life on earth."

"You think I should spare them that disillusionment?" I was glad to be getting some divine counsel for my investment.

"Oh, what the hell," he said. "You might as well tell them the truth. Gould is right in saying *homo sapiens* is a very dangerous animal just because of your intelligence. You are an aberration. Eighty percent of multicellular life enjoys evolutionary success without posing the dangers you humans do. The most successful mammals, in terms of numbers and spread, in terms your computers can quantify, are rats, bats, and antelope. But, of course, the most successful life form is the bacteria. It is the bacteria that survived the massive extinctions of life on the planet. The bacteria just keep on keeping on. In fact there may be bacteria deep inside the earth's crust that get their energy from the heat of the earth's core. As it was in the beginning, bacteria are and ever will be, world without end. Amen."

"So maybe we humans should be a little less arrogant, a little more appropriately humble?"

He looked at me as an adult looks at a child who has just grasped an adult concept. "That's what we gods have been trying to teach you all this time. Limits! Hubris!"

"Thanks. I guess." I felt so bad I didn't even want another lemon-filled, sugar-coated donut. "Coyote," I wailed, "it's hopeless!"

"Oh, cheer up, for God's sake, if not your own. Of course it's hopeless. But you're not going to make it any better by crying in your coffee."

"You mean I should accept that it's hopeless?"

"Well," he said, and I could tell the artful dodger was about to swerve. "Well, I wouldn't want you to give up. This is a stage you have to go through." He looked at me seriously. When someone with big sharp teeth and yellow eyes looks at me seriously, I listen. This is what I heard:

"Freud observed that all the major revolutions of science have involved the successive dethronement of human arrogance. You can understand why people don't like science. We had the Copernican revolution, the Darwinian revolution, the Freudian revolution. Now we have a fourth revolution: the discovery of the deep time of the universe and the age of the earth. The earth is billions of years old. Humans are only part of the latest micro-moment of planetary time. You humans are a momentary cosmic accident that would never arise again if time were rerun. But this goes against the deepest social and psychological beliefs of Western culture. So what do you do? You tell the Darwinian story with a spin that says there is such a thing as progress, and the point of progress is you! Progress is a delusion based on social prejudice engendered by your refusal to accept the implications of deep time. If the tree of life were grown again from seed, it would not produce the same tree. Why not? Because conditions would be different. Evolving life would have to compensate for the different conditions, thus creating different conditions, which would affect the direction of what evolves. There are limits to the complexity that can be handled. You are the small tail on very large dog. As an arrogant tail, you think you have the right to wag the dog."

I was silent. He looked at his tail, which kept its place, knowing better than to try to wag him.

"Thanks," I said. "You really know how to cheer a human up!"

"Oh," he said, "you don't need to worry about whether or not life will survive on the planet. The bacteria are very successful!"

"Stop trying to comfort me!" I yelled. *"You are the least comforting god I have ever had!"*

"But, baby," he crooned, "now you know once again whose responsibility it is if you humans are going to survive."

"Thank you for nothing!" I said. I was about to storm out of the donut shop and leave him with the bill. Except you can't abandon your god just because he tells you the truth.

We sat there in silence. Coyote is a good counselor. He can just sit with me while I struggle with the insights that come out of the relationship. He never tells me what to do.

"Have a fresh cup of coffee," he said. "You'll feel better!"

"Thanks," I said. The waitress replaced my stained and chilled cup with a gleaming white one filled with a steaming, fragrant tonic that smelled like life in a television commercial. Once again, I felt the apple of the universe's eye. It is so sweet to be deluded.

I said, "I watched the president speak recently."

"You were born to suffer," he said.

"I find it depressing, Coyote, that someone so smart thinks the world's problems will be cured by exporting Americanism. I find it especially depressing that what our maximal leader offers the world is consumerism—making the world safe for international corporations. I'm not as anti-business as some of my parishioners think I am. I try to run the church and my personal life in a more or less businesslike manner. But the president seems to miss totally the environmental crisis. Not that he had the wrong answers. He didn't even recognize it as a problem. He is young and intelligent and powerful; the best of his generation."

"Ooh," said Coyote, "glad I don't have TV."

"It's not eco-fascism, but it does involve limits on everyone's being able to do whatever they can get away with in the short run."

He swung around on his stool and addressed the donut shop, which was full of coyotes hiding behind discarded newspapers while warming their paws on their coffee mugs.

"Do you know about the tragedy of the commons?" he asked.

All the coyotes nodded sadly.

"Tell me about the tragedy of the commons," I said.

"In olden times in New Mexico, as in your native New England, there were common pastures. If everyone put three cows to pasture, everyone was equal. Except that one farmer put in four, because he saw he would get more milk, and his family would grow stronger and wealthier. So another farmer put in a fourth cow in order to keep up. Then another farmer put in five to get ahead. Pretty soon the common pasture was overgrazed. The urge for advantage put an end to the commons."

"Why couldn't they legislate it at three cows apiece?"

"Eco-fascist!" he snapped, and all the coyotes laughed at me.

Coyote continued, "You believe the world is overpopulated, yes?"

"Yes, because the death rate has gone down; because people live longer."

"So that's bad, right?"

I could see what was coming, so I shut up.

He went on, "Why do you exercise three times a week? Why do you take your vitamins? Why do you eat your broccoli?"

"So I'll live longer."

"The tragedy of the commons."

"Cut it out!" I said. "If you're offered a longer life, it's just natural to take it."

"That's what the farmer who put another cow to graze thought. That's what the corporations think when they buy a favorable government policy. That's what the private landowner thinks when the government restricts his use of his land."

Sinking lower in my own estimation, I asked, "What's the solution?"

"Be a spiritual leader! Show the courage of your beliefs! Commit suicide!"

"Coyote! Be reasonable! I don't want to commit suicide. I want to live to be a healthy 110-year-old."

"I know. I hope you do. It's just that your awareness and your natural urges are contradictory. If you were an ordinary animal, you wouldn't have this problem. Nature would trim your tree for you."

I'll tell you that Social Security looks better all the time when I'm working for the kind of god a small local Unitarian Universalist congregation can afford. A decent god would appear in thunder and fire to the CEOs of all the world's multinational corporations and say, "You better start tithing to some reforestation projects or everyone who does business with you will develop boils!" Old Moses, now, he could strike terror into a head of state when his god spoke. I thought, we need a new god who can come up with some new commandments and the awe to enforce them.

Coyote read my mind and replied, "The old *deus ex machina* stories don't work anymore. The magic is gone out of them. You humans can't believe anymore that you were created to lord it over the planet. You can't believe anymore that you are the end product of a beautiful process of evolution. Some of you believe you are spirits trapped in flesh and bone, and you will leave this screwed-up world for a mythical plane with no tough decisions anymore, just beautiful, low-level, continuous, spiritual orgasms. Many intelligent humans have given up their childlike faith in technology as a cure-all. Whatever the magic, there are real limits, baby! There are no magical solutions! The real limits have to be taken seriously!"

I smiled resignedly. "I was at our local Ministerial Alliance. One of the ministers said he'd like a program on what various denominations thought of the apocalypse. What was our story of the end of time? I said the Unitarians used to believe in the progress of humanity onward and upward forever. We all had a good laugh at that quaint myth. The next day I read an article about meteorites hitting the earth. The earth's surface is as pock-marked with as many hits as the moon. It's just that we don't see the pockmarks on the earth because the earth's surface has moved and subducted and eroded and is covered with trees and water. The message is that the cosmos is a dangerous place. The story of the end has not been scripted. It will be irrelevant to our wishes."

Coyote squirmed on his stool, then said, "You have to reject any meanings or solutions that come from outside you. If sanity is going to happen, it's going to have to happen from inside you. You can't expect to be rescued from your private and social follies by magic. You have to rely on yourselves or take the consequences."

"Coyote," I said, "is there any hope for that to happen?"

"Why, of course," he said. "Of course there's hope!"

Then he shook himself and looked concerned. "I told Doña Coyote I'd do some errands in town, and look at the time! Let's continue this tomorrow."

So we agreed to meet again in my study.

The next afternoon I was in my study when a glow appeared at each end of my sofa. The two glows materialized into Coyote and Doña Coyote. Coyote looked embarrassed.

"Coyote didn't want me to come," Doña Coyote said matter-of-factly.

Coyote grimaced.

"But I insisted," she said.

I didn't have any trouble believing that. I went into my defensive sensitivity mode, as is wise when doing relationship counseling. Doña Coyote read my thoughts and said, "This is not about Coyote's and my relationship!"

Coyote looked at her skeptically.

"Well," she said, "it's sort of about our relationship. But it's really about Coyote and your church. If he would just stop hanging out at the Unitarian Universalist congregation, things would be much better between us."

Sarcastically, Coyote muttered, "Just do it your way, eh?"

"No, Coyote," she said sweetly, "just do it the right way!"

Coyote slumped lower in the sofa and looked at his knees.

"Doña Coyote," I asked, "in what way is this church interfering in your relationship?"

"Your optimism," she said.

"Our optimism?" I repeated, surprised. "I was just meditating on what a grim future we have with Congress doing away with all the optimistic liberal gains we had made. Not to mention the population explosion and the rich getting richer."

"That's my point!" she said with a logic that escaped me. "That's just my point! The evidence is right before your eyes that life is tragic, but you Unitarian Universalists keep trying to make it sound as if everything could be worked out if we all would just try harder."

"I agree the UUs are guilty of being optimistic," I said, trying to be fair and calming. It only encouraged her.

"It's a false religion!" she said angrily. "Pessimism is what's called for!"

Coyote broke in, saying, "I try to tell her I am only trying to convert the UUs to the joys of pessimism and cynicism, those realistic and comforting doctrines of the natural world and the way things are."

Doña Coyote was angry. "It's dangerous to mess around with error, Coyote. You know you've been harboring some secret optimistic thoughts after this man stuffs you with donuts. You think maybe the future could be a great big, rosy, jelly donut!"

"That's just for the short term," he replied. "Until I get hungry again, my pet."

"Don't call me your pet," she said. "If anyone's become a pet, it's you with your sugar-coated tongue!"

"Doña Coyote," I said, "please tell me what you mean when you say the truth of life is tragedy, pessimism, and cynicism?"

She looked at me suspiciously. "You mean you really don't know?"

It is wise to adopt a conciliatory attitude when confronted with an angry female deity, no matter how minor. I said, "I think I need to hear what you have to say to me."

"You Unitarian Universalists are a moral Corps of Engineers. You insist on bringing in your bulldozers of optimism and reasonable-

ness and convenience and scrape away centuries of mythic consolation for life's tragedies. The surface layer is the consolation
provided by Christianity. Below that in spiritual archeology is the
Native American spiritual layer, which says the sun cannot travel
across the sky without a human death to send it along its way. All
those wonderful religious insights came out of the experience of
living humans, the reality of life's beautiful hardship, the search for
solace in the pain. You want to replace that ancient, wild, spiritual
beauty with some shallow, cheap optimism about the future!"

She looked at me to see how I was taking it. I said nothing, which
she considered an encouraging sign. She went on. "Look at the
evidence around you. Look at the abandoned cave dwellings at
Bandelier. Look at Chaco Canyon, abandoned after they wore out
the environment. Look at Mesa Verde. You call those a basis for
optimism about the future?"

I found my courage at last. I said, "Yes, the evidence is there that
human civilization is a fragile thing. Humans should treat the
environment with caution or our cities will end up like Chaco
Canyon. But we UUs don't say, 'Well, it can't be helped.' We say,
'Let's look at the past as a model for the future and acknowledge
how fragile the environment is—'"

She interrupted, "Don't try to tell me you UUs have learned anything. I don't see your congregation riding bicycles or buses!"

She had me cold.

"And don't start telling me you want to make Santa Fe a better
place to live. You move here and then complain how backward it
is, and how you want to make it progressive like Boston or Los
Angeles."

"Doña Coyote!" I said, outraged. "Look at the high school drop-
out rate! Do you think we can sit around and do nothing? New
Mexico is headed for fiftieth in childhood poverty! Progressive
ideas are compassionate ideas, Doña Coyote. Justice is a religious
commitment from Old Testament times."

"Progressive ideas just make things worse," she said. "Compassion comes from realizing the tragic character of our lives, that
we need solace. Your progressive optimism ignores the awful

brevity and fragility of every life and tries to make people think everyone should have a sweet, bland, trouble-free, technology-enhanced life! Life itself as it is is not fair. How can there be any justice in nature?"

"Not true, Doña Coyote! Not true! Our gospel is that people can take charge of their lives, and collectively. Through responsibility and reasonableness and cooperation we can build a better life. We believe in modesty and education and justice. We want to make this life better, Doña Coyote. This is the only life we get, despite the empty promises of some of your fellow gods. Yes, of course there is tragedy, but we still think we can make life better decade by decade. We think that's what life is about: compassion and justice and progress."

Doña Coyote indicated Coyote with a flip of her paw. "Look at him. He's what life's about. Lies, seductions, tricks, petty greed, cheating, gambling, getting fat, hunting, goofing off. He enjoys life!"

Coyote responded with a big grin, a shrug, and an adoring look at Doña Coyote. She responded with a soulful, amused, loving, exasperated look. I thought to myself that these two sure don't need my counseling.

Once again she read my thoughts.

"Of course we don't need your counseling. We're natural creatures. We know and accept the dark side of life as well as the beauty of trotting across the desert at sunrise. We coyotes are the gods of disorder who subvert the business ethic that is constantly trying to get everything organized and predictable. We coyotes know about getting it wrong and paying the consequences. Sometimes we suffer when we don't deserve to, but we never sue. People are glad to hear about our vital spirit that keeps us going despite all life's painful blows and tricks and limitations. That's life, right? We coyotes sing about life. We tell tales of life's tragedy and irony and fun. Because we know all that, when life is good and our bellies are full, well, we just smile and enjoy. You would take all that away and replace it with reasonableness and virtue and air conditioning for all."

Coyote finally spoke up. "My dear," he said, and his voice was quiet and respectful, but full of courage. "My dear, these humans are evolving. They are learning new things. They have abandoned relying on prayer to save them. They are trying new ways of living together. I know the people of this little congregation. They are gentle with each other while arguing about all the gutsy stuff humans deal with. In their hearts, they respect each other's souls. They are empowering and compassionate. They open their minds and their arms to embrace each other and life. They listen. I admit they don't sing as well as we do, but they have other ways of sharing their gladness in each other. I think they are evolving."

"See?" she said to me. "He's become an optimist hanging out here!"

Coyote shrugged. "Maybe it's the novelty of it. I like hope in conscious beings."

"I told you you'd get addicted to civilization," she said. "The easy fantasy life, that's my Coyote!"

"Doña, my love, these humans have some good ideas. We know from ancient experience that we think the best reaction to life's tragedies is to play the fool. But there have been coyotes for a long, long time. We do not worry about the ultimate survival of coyotes. What will be will be. But we do not stick up our noses at the dregs of human civilization. We did not invent warm places where humans can gather and enjoy donuts and coffee and good conversation about ideas. But Doña, my dear, these humans have not only invented donut shops, they have invented better social systems to replace their old social systems. I have noticed these Unitarian Universalists experimenting with new ways of running their organization. For instance, their alpha male here cannot give orders but must be a non-judgmental facilitator."

I had never been identified as an alpha male before. The concept pleased me. My mind wandered to the pleasant possibilities, so I only got the barest gist of Coyote's argument that the Unitarian Universalists, with a little help from the Green Party, were at the cutting edge of a kinder gentler civilization. I came back at a lull in their conversation.

"Doña Coyote," I said, "perhaps both points of view are correct."

"No!" she said. "We cannot both be correct!"

My new alpha male identity kicked in, and I amazed the three of us by saying, "Look, this is my office, my turf. I say we can contradict and still both be right. The truth is much too big for any of us to encompass. It is true that life is tragic and glorious at the same time, sometimes in the same moment. It is also true that in the short term, progress can be made as people become more intelligent. As people get more insight into their own motivations and the way the human culture serves or doesn't serve those motivations, they can control the wilder flights of their personal aggrandizement. As we understand and accept the limits of our mother earth, we shall learn to have the same affection as we once had for the Sky God of Moses. What's more, we understand that the evolutionary civilizing process is not automatic and upward forever. It takes humans to make it work. It takes organized humans to make it work. The outcome is not guaranteed, but there is a record of progress in the short years of human history. It will take a planetary consensus that the planet is our commons, and we must limit our human desire to get an inordinate share of the commons. And even that may not be enough, sad as it is to tell. But we can try to use our intelligence."

Doña Coyote drew a sharp breath and said to Coyote "Well, sniff the alpha male!"

"I have sniffed the whole congregation, my dear, and I find their ideals and vision wonderful. The real reason I hang out with them is not that I believe as they do, but I want to encourage their trickster possibilities. Humans are unpredictable. That gives them hope. Entropy will get us nothing in the end, as it has countless other universes. For the moment, though, I find humans fascinating and hopeful, tricksters like us. Humans keep answering the questions we gods know shouldn't even be asked. We know life should accept life as it is. But these humans keep asking questions about what life is for and how they can make it better for more people. They think that is the answer to the unanswerable question of why there are humans."

"But, Coyote!" she said. "Their answers are always wrong!"

"So what?" he said. "They're trying. They're trying to figure out the good life. Not just any old life, but the good life. We think we know that life has no purpose other than having fun and taking the consequences, raising the pups. But these humans have the effrontery to try to figure out how to make life more glorious."

I decided to get in on the glorious onslaught. "Doña Coyote, we are alone and unprotected by the gods. We are without an operating manual in a dangerous cosmos. The future is uncertain except that we know we personally must die and that sometime the planet must die. We have to find ways of getting along with humans we don't like much as well as getting along with the humans we love. We are storytellers, we humans. We live by our stories. We are starting to tell a new story of the cosmos, and how it came to be. We are starting to tell a new story of how planet earth became such a beautiful and rich place. We are starting to tell a new story of humanity—an adventure in freedom of the spirit in open democratic societies. We hope our new story also tells of physical science and social science saving us from a future that looks so grim. Even with the earth's limits, which are a part of the new story, we can still try to live by this new story that life is a grand adventure. Perhaps with intelligence and awareness we can self-limit ourselves and also do justice and love mercy."

We three sat quietly for a moment, and then Doña Coyote said, "Well, my damn fool lover boy knows you better than I do. I still think you get the prize for arrogance, thinking you can improve on what the gods created. But OK, keep trying! If you pull it off, I'll turn in my trickster credentials and eat your donuts."

And with that, she dematerialized.

Coyote laughed, and said, "I won't go to Houston with you, so I turned on your word processor, and it recorded the whole thing. Just read them the transcript. Tell them there's hope. Humans have to have hope to live."

He, too, disappeared, and I quickly saved and printed this document before Doña Coyote found out about it!

COYOTE CAN'T RETIRE

was reading a *Dilbert* cartoon. First, the boss says, "We're not giving any raises." Then the boss says, "We think work is its own reward." Then the boss says, "Expect to be rewarded twice as much next year!"

At which point Coyote appeared. He shook his head, bared his teeth, and flattened his ears. He said, "I hear you are retiring. You can't retire."

"Yes, I can," I said. "They've already wished us well. We're committed."

"Why didn't you tell me?" he demanded.

"They all say you're a creature of my imagination," I said. "Why would I tell you? You know all my most intimate secrets."

"Here we go again," he said. "You imagine you imagine me. I know I imagine you. You imagine! I know! That's the difference between a human and a god."

"Well, then," I said, "if I am only imagining I imagine you, then you must have known I would imagine I imagine you, so it's your own fault if I am wrongly imagining that I imagine you."

He said resignedly, "I imagine so. I'm never going to convince you that you're not real."

"And," I said, "I'm never going to convince the congregation that you're real. They think all gods are a figment of human imagination."

"We are," he said calmly.

"But you just said you imagine us!" I said, frustrated by this conversation.

He said, "We imagine each other. It's mind magic. In the gods you create a mirror for yourselves onto which you project your favorite selves. You tell stories about us gods that allow you to see yourselves more clearly. You get a little perspective on yourselves. Bounce your image off the mystery out there and then pick up incoming echoing messages."

I said, "Let's go over to GI Joe's Coffee Shop and discuss this over sweet rolls."

He said, "I'll buy. It's a retirement present."

When we had the sweet rolls, six for Coyote and one for me, and two coffees, Coyote dug a coin out of a secret place where he keeps things, not having pockets, and put it on the counter.

"What's that?" asked the counter woman.

"That's to pay for our sweet rolls and coffee," said Coyote. "Keep the change."

"That's a quarter," said the counter woman. "You just got $16.35 worth of sweet rolls and coffee."

"Close enough," said Coyote.

The counter woman said, "You know, it's things like this that make dogs unwelcome in stores."

Coyote said to me, "Tell her who I am!"

"He's Coyote," I said, "the famous Native American minor deity." I slipped her a twenty. But Coyote had already gathered up the sweet rolls and headed for the table. I had protected him from the real world of humans once again. He was serenely oblivious.

"Thanks for buying!" I said as I sat down.

"It's the least I could do," he said, and I silently agreed with him.

"Am I going to have to find a new mouthpiece?" he asked.

"Well," I said, "you could retire with me. It would leave the world a less interesting place without your tricks."

"That's why I can't retire," he said. "I have to be here to explain things people feel there's no explanation for."

"Like the Navajo stories of why people die and why the stars are every which way."

"Yes," he said. "People need explanations for life not being reasonable and orderly, so they make them up. They publish their explanations, and people say, 'Oh, so that's why it's the way it is.' The people who made up the explanation become convinced because it's so believable that they forget they made it up."

"That's your version of theology?" I asked.

"Can you think of a better way to express it?" he asked

"I can see it in some fields, like the *meaning* of being human, that human knowing is best expressed in stories. But surely not in science. Science and reason deal with real stuff!"

"If it weren't for things unexplainable, there would be no need to do science," he said. "Science is fun because of the tricks and traps waiting for the curious researcher. That keeps scientists on the edge of their seats. Scientists tell discovery stories that give their lives meaning."

"Progress," I said.

"Well," he said, "calling it progress puts a complimentary value judgment on it. I suppose you would call that story of the first people and me deciding whether there would be death in the world a myth, a legend, an explanation made up by a primitive people. The Navajos looked at reality, and though they didn't want to die any more than anyone else does, they could see the necessity of death if people kept on having babies. There would soon be only standing room on the planet. The Navajo story is more intelligent than the position of the U.S. Congress which won't allow U.S. funds to be used for family planning information. The Navajo story is more intelligent than medical science which keeps people alive and refuses to let them die with dignity until all their money is gone. The Navajos recognized the situation as a cruel trick, but they could understand the why of it and accept it. You super-bright people believe Archer Daniels Midland, supermarket to the world, is going to save you from the benefits of your own technology."

"A coyote trick on the modern world," I said. "Why don't you retire, Coyote? Haven't you done enough damage? Why don't you let us poor humans be?"

"*I can't retire! I'm immortal!*" he said. "I've tried to retire, but reality won't let me. I am tired of keeping humans off balance. They never appreciate what I do to make their life interesting and fun. They don't know their sense of aliveness and adventure comes from me! But if I leave them for even a little while they complain about how boring life has become. They are so demanding. They need to complain to their friends, 'Oh, life really threw me a curve yesterday. Let me tell you!' But do I get appreciated? Never. Except for you, my friend." He began to sniffle. "You understand me. You know what a cruel eternal existence I've been handed."

I handed him my handkerchief and he honked into it and wiped his eyes.

I said, "So your tricks about the shortness of life are to show us how brief the sweetness is?"

"Yes," he said. "So you will not be bored by life, but will accept the glory and joy of the universe right now, which you have been freely given by the universe."

I said, "But we think it's all an accident, a meaningless accident."

He shook his head in wonder. "Think that if you will. Maybe your human species really is an accident. But your human conscious-ness of beauty and pleasure is still a miracle, a grace-filled life which you were given, yet have to take the action of accepting."

We sat there quietly and contemplated the grace-filled gift of friendship.

Then he smiled and said, "Do you suppose we could get just a few more of those sweet rolls? I'm afraid I don't have another quarter!"

I sighed and got up. The counter woman said, "Something more for your dog?"

I said, "I told you he's a god, not a dog. G-o-d, not d-o-g."

She smiled and said, "You're nearer your god than me."

I said, "He walks with me and he talks with me and he tells me I am his own."

She said, "Be careful what joys you share as you tarry there."

"Oh," I said, "I've been warned by skeptics about that."

"Well," she leaned over and whispered, "you're no crazier than the others who come in here. But you look like you're having fun with your dog."

"God," I said.

"Yeah," she said. "Have it your way. You're the customer!"

I returned to the table with more sweet rolls and coffee.

Coyote looked at me and said, "You spent a lot of time with that young woman. What was going on?"

I said, "Oh, she wanted your phone number."

"I don't have a phone," he said.

"I know," I said. "I told her you were in very high-level diplomatic work and had an unlisted phone. I said you might surprise her someday."

"Yes," he said, "I think I will."

"So," I said, "maybe you're just not ready to retire after all. Maybe there are other humans you have to do your little life tricks on?"

"My work is cut out for me," he said. "So many humans, so little time. I am afraid I miss some of them and they escape to live uneventful lives. They don't appreciate the miracle of having a mind."

I said, "Whatever that is."

"A mind is a trick of the imagination," he said. "The human mind doesn't exist, yet we know it exists."

"Like the soul," I said.

"Yes," he said. "There is no such thing, yet it exists as a quality of being."

"Like God," I said.

"Oh, your nasty skeptic side is showing," he said. "Can't you hold it in for another week, for God's sake?"

"Coyote," I said, "I can be a trickster, too. I can be as strict a skeptic as anyone and be open about it, too, for there's nothing to fear about being a skeptic other than the possibility of being wrong. There's nothing wrong with being wrong. Yet the reverse is also true. There's nothing to fear about believing that God is good except that you might be wrong and thus be unprepared for a nasty Coyote surprise."

He reflected a moment, and then he asked meditatively, "Is that a trick I'm playing on you, or is that a trick you're playing on me?"

"Both," I said.

"It's like the imagining thing," he said.

"Let's not get into that again," I said.

He grinned. "The human mind, which some believe doesn't exist since it can't be quantified, is a wonderful event in time and space, having consequences and effects. You imagine me and I imagine you and it's coffee for thee and donuts for me, and me for you and you for me, and can't you see how happy we could *be!*"

He began to howl. People came out from behind their news-papers. I couldn't help myself; I began to howl with the joy of it, too. Pretty soon the other patrons were up and doing the old soft shoe. The counter woman sang, "No one is near us to see us or hear us!" Coyote grinned at her and sang, "They don't even know that we have a telephone."

We were all singing "Me for you and you for me and can't you see how happy …!" when the door opened and a policeman came in. The policeman shouted, "Stop it! I am the Voice of Reason. You're all under arrest!"

The patrons jumped behind their newspapers. Coyote and I started playing checkers. The counter woman rearranged the pastries. "That's better," said the blue-uniformed Voice of Reason.

Then the Voice of Reason chuckled and said, "I understand. You're only human. I forgive you!" And everything would have been cool except that Coyote snorted a derisive snort.

"I heard that," said the Voice of Reason.

"You can't arrest me," said Coyote. "I'm a god. I'm the Trickster. I'm above human laws."

"You have to submit to the Laws of Reasonableness," said the policeman. "You are a figment of human imagination."

Coyote was not to be stopped. "I admit to being a figment of human imagination, but at least I give them a good time. You, friend officer, are a trickster keeping them from their full animal emotional needs."

"You must respect my authority," said the Voice of Reason.

Coyote turned to me, and his eyes flashed. "What was that car-toon you summoned me with?" he asked. "Tell it to the Voice of Reason."

I said, "Well, the boss said, 'We're not giving raises. We think work is its own reward. Expect to be rewarded about twice as much next year.'"

The Voice of Reason thought a moment and then said gravely, "That seems reasonable!"

"You see," said Coyote, "why I can't retire?"

We embraced. The counter woman embraced the patrons of GI Joe's Coffee Shop. We did a conga line toward the door.

"Hey," said the policeman. "Don't you guys want to be arrested? It's for your own good!"

"Tell it to the judge!" I said.

The policeman was puzzled. "What judge?" he asked.

Coyote laughed. "Gotcha!" he cried. "Reason serves its masters: human passion and self-interest."

I said, "Reason also serves compassion and understanding."

Coyote said, "When it does, that's where grace and mystery meet."

"Neat trick, Coyote," I said.

He grinned widely and said, "It's all in your imagination."

I grinned and said, "I don't believe you!"